THE FROZEN
HORS-D'OEUVRE COOKBOOK

You've Got It Made!

THE
FROZEN
HORS-D'OEUVRE
COOKBOOK

You've Got It Made!

by

Jane Keyes

Illustrations by Jane Breit

HASTINGS HOUSE · PUBLISHERS

New York, N.Y. 10016

Library of Congress Cataloging in Publication Data

Keyes, Jane.
    The frozen hors-d'oeuvre cookbook.

    Includes index.
    1. Cookery (Appetizers)   2. Cookery (Frozen foods)
I. Title.
TX740.K49   1980   641.8'12   80-36676
ISBN 0-8038-8602-0

Published simultaneously in Canada by
Saunders of Toronto, Ltd., Don Mills, Ontario
Designed by Al Lichtenberg
Printed in the United States of America

for
H.M.K.

CONTENTS

Introduction   9
Bases and Basics   17
    Metrics   17
    Equipment   19
    How to Freeze and Thaw Hors-d'Oeuvre   21
    Breads and Pastries for Canapé and
        Hors-d'Oeuvre Bases   23
    To Use Recipes as Spreads or Dips   38
    Garnishes   38
Cheeses   41
Fish and Shellfish   61
Chicken   95
Meats   111
Vegetables   141
Sauces   163
Cocktail-Buffet   171
Receptions (Champagne, Punch, Eggnog,
    Tea or Coffee Parties)   189

Index   209

INTRODUCTION

"Hello, been to Portland, have you?" This was the friendly greeting I received from the plump, affable proprietress of a combination grocery and newspaper store in a small town in Maine where I live. The reason for her deduction was that I was wearing a hat and earrings. Everyone in this part of Maine knows that when you are dressed in such a fashion, on a beautiful fall day, you have been to a Hospital League luncheon or a meeting of your bridge club, or you have just returned from a shopping expedition to Portland—providing, of course, that it isn't Sunday and you might have been to church. Otherwise you would have been in your customary jeans.

We live in a gentle place—quiet, but far from sleepy. There are many attractive and sophisticated people living in this part of Maine year-round. In the summer it becomes less quiet and the tourists and summer people "from away" swell our ranks considerably. These people and my family and friends are directly responsible for my start in an hors-d'oeuvre business, the last thing that I ever would have expected to do.

My paternal grandmother was a superior cook who wrote many small, but choice cookbooks. Unfortunately, only one little gem seems to have survived over the years. (We've been a family of nomads!) My mother, too, is an exceptional cook. I have inherited my love for cooking from these two ladies.

Making hors-d'oeuvre is, for me, a great fun thing to do. I love fixing for my guests platters of canapés both hot and cold, arranged as attractively as I can make them. It is a challenge and a satisfaction to me to create new ones for each party.

On occasion I have helped friends when they have had large Christmas or anniversary parties. The result of this was their urging me to sell my hors-d'oeuvre so that they could have them whenever they wanted them. I didn't think that I would be able to do it until it occurred to me to freeze them. My children were grown up so I had plenty of time to experiment with this new idea.

We have an excellent specialty shop that caters to gourmets in the surrounding towns. I finally did sell my hors-d'oeuvre there, but not before I'd had a few amusing and embarrassing episodes.

After months of experimenting to find out what foods froze well and what would definitely flop, I felt ready to enter into, what seemed to me at the time, the glamorous world of business and to try to market my hors-d'oeuvre and canapés. An ad the following week in the local paper, giving my name and telephone number, archly said, "COCKTAILS ANYONE??? HAPPY TO MAKE YOUR HORS-D'OEUVRE FOR YOU! JUST CALL—etcetera, etcetera." I shudder when I think of the nonsense in my ads in the weeks that followed.

The local paper comes out on Thursday. I cut out an enormous sheet of paper to hang on the wall by the phone that first day, expecting a constant stream of calls. It had lists of hors-d'oeuvre with their descriptions and prices so that, when the phone rang, the efficiency of my new business would be instantly apparent to any prospective customer.

Days went by. Weeks went by. Even though the house was always occupied and the phone constantly tended, there were no calls for hors-d'oeuvre. Finally I stopped the ads, took the huge hors-d'oeuvre list down, and put it away. There didn't seem to be much point in having my potential business go into the red before it even got off the ground!

Five weeks after my first ad had appeared, I got the first telephone call. WHERE is the paper with my LISTS? Where is ANY paper?? Why is there NEVER a pencil by the phone?? What kind of hors-d'oeuvre DO I make anyway??? After my spluttering and babbling through a few recipes from memory and trying to sound like a graduate of Le Cordon Bleu (with little success), this marvelous, trusting woman ordered TWO HUNDRED canapés for a cocktail party five days hence. I was in business!

Before I became associated with a store, the packaging of the frozen canapés and delivery to my customers was rather tricky. The canapés were placed on paper doilies on paper plates, artistically arranged and decorated with parsley, nasturtium leaves, watercress, or some other pretty garnish. Another plate was inverted over them and taped in place. Stacks of these were put in the trunk of my car. Then began the nerve-wracking trip to town: Every pothole and bump in the road must be studiously avoided but I had to keep in mind the thought that time was of the essence, since I was supposed to be delivering FROZEN hors-d'oeuvre. A sudden start or stop might transfer a bit of caviar to the pickled onion or a ripe olive to the sherried shrimp, which would be the ruination of all of my efforts.

Once in town, I made my way to the parking lot behind the stores where my culinary masterpieces were proudly and tenderly transferred to the trunk of my customer's car. With a sigh of relief and money in my pocket, I headed home feeling much more like a street vendor than a queen of the kitchen.

That first order brought five more the following day from people who had attended the cocktail party the night before. As my list of customers grew, so did my reputation and I felt bold enough to approach the owner of the food specialty store. Providing that I could arrange a different and more compact packaging system, she would be delighted to carry my hors-d'oeuvre in her freezer. I did. And she did. The result was that we had a happy and mutually profitable association for more than six years. I might still be working at it but the owner of the store retired and I remarried.

My wonderful family and loyal friends have urged me to write down and share my recipes. So here they are, with a reminder that nearly all of them are my own. From time to time I have acquired a few from friends, tried them, and adapted them to the freezer. From an economic angle, they are far less expensive to make than to buy.

My "Test Kitchen"

Have you ever read in the food magazines sold in our supermarkets the phrase, "developed in our own test kitchen?" Some of the more popular home magazines have also come out with their own versions of the same phrase, "kitchen-tested recipes," "foolproof recipes from our own test kitchens," and other such descriptive phrases. This is a formidable and sobering thought for one who has decided to write a cookbook.

One has the mental picture of many white-garbed women with stern and uncompromising faces trying out a recipe that must, if it is to appear in their magazine, be 100% everything—foolproof, delicious, gorgeous to look at, photogenic and cheap!

In the quest of providing this book with recipes which have similar qualifications, I have gone into my "test kitchen." Most of the time I seem to have lying on my feet, singly or in pairs, two large Chesapeake Bay Retrievers, except when they are joined by their adopted brother, a huge Labrador Retriever. When that happens, there is a general free-for-all and the hors-d'oeuvre experiments come to a halt until they can all be shooed outside. You can see how this kind of activity in a "test kitchen" would hamper the creativity and productivity of the cook somewhat.

We have occasional frozen pipes in the winter, a vegetable garden 100 x 75 feet in the summer, and we get the harvest into the freezer in the fall. In spite of the dogs and our happily hectic lifestyle, I have managed to collect my recipes for hors-d'oeuvre and canapés that I sold in the store for so many years and incorporate them in this book. I hope that they will measure up favorably to the far more scientifically tested recipes printed in home magazines.

I hope that what you find will intrigue you, but even more that these recipes will stimulate your own inventiveness and serve as an incentive for you to experiment. Make some hors-d'oeuvre on a rainy day when you have a party in the offing, and stash them away in your freezer. Then when you come back from Portland, or wherever you are, in a smashing new hat and silver earrings, and yearning for a dry martini with canapés, "YOU'VE GOT IT MADE!"

THE FROZEN
HORS-D'OEUVRE COOKBOOK

You've Got It Made!

BASES
AND BASICS

Metrics

The metric system seems to be coming into our lives at a rapid rate. A lot of people aren't ready for it yet. In fact, some friends of mine have told me that they don't think they will ever be ready for it. I am going to try to get these skeptics in a more receptive mood and see that the metric system is not so formidable after all.

I took the problem of attempting to convert my book to metrics to the National Bureau of Standards in Washington, D.C. They sent me all manner of conversion charts and metric tables and, to my utter amazement, they were understandable, even to me. In hopes of helping the cook-hostess, in culinary matters at least, I'm giving the recipes in this book in the old familiar measurements with the conversion to metrics as well. Fortunately, in hors-d'oeuvre cookery there aren't too many to learn. Perhaps with the old *and* new measurements in the same recipe, it won't be long before you have picked up the mass, volume and temperature measurements with little effort. If I can do it, anyone can.

So, with this book in hand, how about going off to the kitchen and whipping up some unusual hors-d'oeuvre for tonight or for two weeks from tonight? Think what a relaxed cocktail hour you will have serving them to your guests whenever they come, and it will be without any apparent effort on your part.

APPROXIMATE CONVERSIONS
TO METRIC MEASURES

When you know	Multiply by	To find

VOLUME

When you know	Multiply by	To find
fluid ounces	30	milliliters
cups	0.24	liters
pints	0.47	liters
quarts	0.95	liters

MASS (weight)

When you know	Multiply by	To find
ounces	28	grams
pounds	0.45	kilograms

TEMPERATURE (exact)

When you know	Multiply by	To find
Fahrenheit	5/9 (after subtracting 32)	Celsius

Equipment

There are only a few pieces of equipment mentioned in the following list that are not normally found in every household, and even those could be dispensed with. The slotted bread slicer that is shown in the picture (with the biscuit cutters) is a great help in making those very thin slices of bread for ribbon sandwiches. You put a regular slice of bread in it, close it, and slice down from the top. It does a nice even job. If you haven't one or cannot find one, you can do the same thing with a sharp knife, a good eye and a steady hand. The tartlet pans are nice to have but the same little pastries can be baked in a muffin tin; not quite as pretty, but nice just the same.

1. Biscuit, canapé or cooky cutters
2. Slotted bread slicer for making thin slices even thinner
3. Serrated knife
4. Butter spreader
5. Meat grinder or food processor
6. Measuring cups and spoons
7. Cooky or baking sheets, some with raised edges
8. 1-pint (½-liter), 1-quart (1-liter) freezer bags and boxes
9. ½-gallon (2-liter) freezer bags for large quantities
10. Cheese grater
11. Wire whisks
12. Muffin pans
13. Pastry bag or tube, with tips (at least one tip with a ½-inch (1½-centimeter) opening
14. Tartlet pans
15. Egg beater
16. Pie plates
17. Assorted spoons and spatulas
18. Paper towels
19. Colander and strainer

How to Freeze
and Thaw Hors-d'Oeuvre

My freezer is the upright type and will take a large quantity of food, including many trays of hors-d'oeuvre, even if I do have to move things around a little. If you have a minimum of freezer space and want to prepare hors-d'oeuvre in advance for a big party, enlist the help of a friendly neighbor who has a larger freezer with room in it to spare. Make several trays of canapés and take them to his or her house or apartment.

Put all canapés, whether bread, toast, turnovers or pastry rounds in a single layer on a cooky sheet, pie plate, or whatever pan fits best in your freezer space. When frozen hard, put them in 1-quart or 1-pint (1-liter or ½-liter) freezer bags, label them, and replace in the freezer. You can get from 24 to 34 canapés in a quart (liter) bag.

The flavor of a bread round fades more quickly than that of a toast round so I don't usually keep bread rounds longer than 2 to 3 weeks. Turnovers, however, and most other pastries last the longest. Fish canapés are an exception; it is not advisable to keep fish or shellfish canapés more than a couple of weeks. The flavor gets stronger the longer you keep them.

TO THAW BREAD CANAPÉS

It will take 1½ to 2 hours *at room temperature* to thaw bread canapés (the shorter time on a hot summer day).

Remove the frozen hors-d'oeuvre from their packages and arrange them attractively on a serving platter. Cover loosely with very damp paper towels. Fix yourself a "dressing drink" and hop into a warm tub. When you are handsomely dressed, greatly relaxed and refreshed (and your guests are driving up to your front door) poke a bit of greenery among the hors-d'oeuvre and you will suddenly realize what this book is all about. Instant hors-d'oeuvre! And don't forget the cocktail napkins!

TO THAW TOAST CANAPÉS
OR TURNOVERS

You do not need to thaw these, but you can't luxuriate quite as long in a steaming tub. Perhaps you might cut your relaxing time by 5 minutes. Take the hors-d'oeuvre from the freezer and put them on a cooky sheet when the guests are driving up to the door. While your husband is mixing drinks—if you haven't one of these desirable built-in partners, you'll have to work it out for yourself—pop the sheet in the oven preheated to the specified setting. Set the timer for the time recommended in the specific recipe. Don't put on the kitchen fan. The delicious odors will tantalize and delight your guests.

Arrange the hors-d'oeuvre on a platter and garnish with some greenery. Present them to your friends while mentally congratulating yourself on having been foresighted enough to get them made weeks ago.

Breads and Pastries for Canapé and Hors-d'Oeuvre Bases

JUNIPER HILL BREAD

This bread is the one I use most often for my hors-d'oeuvre recipes. It is so easy to make that I recommend it to everyone. It does not have to be kneaded much and is very quick to rise. It will surprise you to find how simple and quick it is.

> ¾ ounce (21 grams) dried yeast
> 3½ cups (8 deciliters) warm water
> ¼ cup (½ deciliter) warm milk
> ¼ cup (½ deciliter) molasses
> 8 cups (1.8 kilograms) unbleached flour
> ⅓ cup (50 grams) whole-wheat or cracked-wheat flour
> 1 tablespoon salt
> ⅓ cup (¾ deciliter) vegetable oil

Turn oven on as low as it will go for 5 minutes, then turn it off. Meanwhile, empty the packages of yeast into a large bowl. Add the warm water, warm milk and the molasses. Stir until the yeast is dissolved. Add 4 cups (.9 kilograms) of the unbleached flour, all the whole-wheat or cracked-wheat flour and the salt. Mix dough well by beating it with a large spoon. Add the rest of the flour and mix it in. When dough gets a bit hard to stir, I usually discard the spoon and use my hands and fingers like an eggbeater. It's sticky but fun. If you don't care for that kind of fun, just keep on with the spoon. It doesn't really take much time. When the flour is all incorporated, add the vegetable oil. Punch dough down with your fist and keep turning it over until oil has been absorbed.

Cover the bowl of dough with plastic wrap and put it in the warm oven to rise. Set the timer for 45 minutes. Dough should be nearly doubled in bulk by that time. Pour it out on a floured board and knead for about 2 minutes. Cut the bread dough into halves with a long knife. Put the halves in 2 buttered loaf pans (9 x 5 x 3 inches or 23 x 13 x 8 centimeters). Turn the oven to 375° F. (190° C.). Cover the pans with plastic wrap and let the dough rise in a warm place outside of the oven for 30 minutes. It should be nearly doubled again. Place pans in the middle of the preheated oven and bake for 30 minutes. Turn out on a rack, put the loaves on their sides, and cover with a towel until cool.

This recipe makes 2 loaves each weighing approximately 2 pounds, 4 ounces (1 kilogram). There are about 30 slices per loaf and each slice makes 6 or 7 bread rounds 1½ inches (4 centimeters) in diameter.

It is a very good, firm bread and an excellent base for the canapés in this book. I hope you will try it. The cost to make this bread is about three times cheaper than the weight-equivalent of store bread. *Storage time (whole): 6 months.*

CANAPÉ ROUNDS:

One of the best uses of this bread dough (other than delicious bread, of course) is to make miniature canapé rounds.

Mix the dough according to the basic directions. After dough has risen once, punch it down, pour out on a floured surface, and knead slightly. Pinch off walnut-size pieces, form them in balls, and put them on a buttered cooky sheet. Some pieces you might roll between the palms until they are about 2 inches long and resemble tiny hot-dog rolls. Cover them with plastic wrap and let them rise until doubled. Bake in a 375° F. (190° C.) oven for 15 minutes. Place them on a rack, cover them with a towel, and let them cool. Slice them horizontally, making 2 canapé rounds out of each one. Freeze them on a cooky sheet or whatever fits your freezer space. When frozen, put the rounds in freezer bags, label, and return to the freezer.

Doing them this way is a great time saver as it eliminates the necessity for cutting out bread rounds from bread slices. The little rounds have a lot of eye and taste appeal when spread with various canapé mixtures.

BREAD ROUNDS AND BASES

The word "rounds" is used loosely throughout this book. The "rounds" can be square, oblong, oval, triangular or crescent shaped. The shape you decide on will undoubtedly be governed by whether you are in a practical or a quixotic mood and whether you have 2 minutes or 2 hours to fool around. Approximate sizes would be a 1¾-inch (4½-centimeter) round, cut with a cooky, canapé or biscuit cutter if you have one. The approximate size of a rectangle, cut with a sharp knife, would be 1¾ inches x 1 inch (4½ x 2½ centimeters).

There are 15 to 18 slices of bread in a standard store loaf (20 plus in a loaf of Juniper Hill bread). You will get 5 rounds or 8 rectangles (crust removed) from a single slice of bread. Therefore you can expect to get 75 to 90 *rounds* and 120 to 144 *rectangles* from a store loaf of bread.

The freshest bread should be used and kudos to you if you baked it yourself. Don't use any of that fluffy, air-filled white stuff that passes for bread in the markets. Use only breads of substance. Try making the Juniper Hill bread; it's easy.

Butter is preferred to "the other spread" but, whichever you use, every round must be spread with it before applying the chosen canapé material. Otherwise you will come up with a soggy mess when the canapés are thawed. Use just enough butter to seal the bread. For each round use ⅛ teaspoon; for the rectangle, the same amount. In every case I have suggested the kind of bread to use but remember that "experiment" is the key word to producing exciting, unusual hors-d'oeuvre.

TOAST ROUNDS AND BASES

Cut out rounds of bread 1¾ inches (4½ centimeters) in diameter with a cooky, canapé or biscuit cutter. If you would like to make another shape, use a sharp knife; after removing the crusts, cut slices into rectangles 1¾ inches x 1 inch (4½ x 2½ centimeters). Make them other shapes if you wish, but keep them in this approximate size.

Place them on a cooky sheet in a preheated 350° F. (180° C.) oven for 5 or 6 minutes, or until they feel slightly dry to the touch but have not taken on any color. If you have a finicky oven, a few experiments will tell you precisely how long to do the rounds.

When they seem done, remove them from the oven, cover them with a dry towel, and allow them to cool. Put them in the freezer in labeled freezer bags. They will keep for at least a month. When spread with some hors-d'oeuvre material, they may even be frozen again. It's great to have a bunch of these on hand.

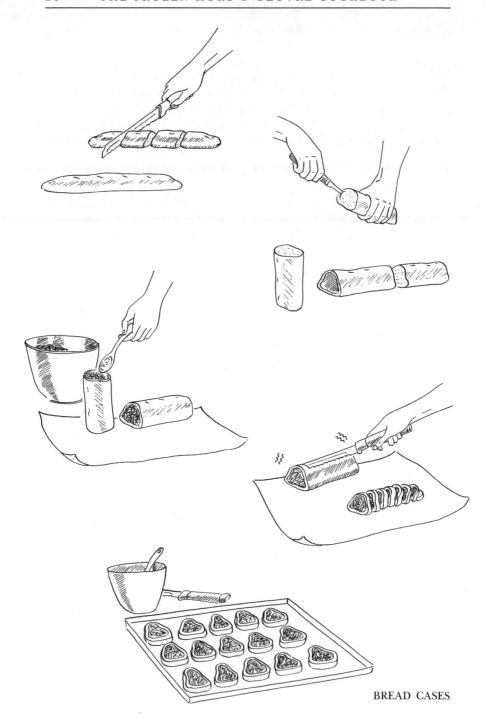

BREAD CASES

BREAD CASES FOR COLD HORS-D'OEUVRE

This is one of the quickest and easiest hors-d'oeuvre bases to make, provided that you live where you can buy those long skinny loaves of French bread. Some people I know are making their own, and with great success.

Buy or make a long thin loaf, no more than 2½ inches (6½ centimeters) in diameter. Cut the ends off and then cut the loaf into 4 pieces. With a fork hollow out the sections, leaving ½-inch (1½-centimeter) shells. These shells may be stuffed with any hors-d'oeuvre mixture that contains butter and/or cream cheese so that when chilled it will harden enough to be sliced. Wrap the rolls in plastic wrap and chill in the refrigerator until the stuffing is very firm. With a sharp, serrated knife, slice them into ½-inch (1½-centimeter) slices. Freeze on a cooky sheet. When frozen, put them in freezer bags, label, and return to the freezer. *One loaf of bread will make about 40 canapés.*

To use: Remove the canapés from the bags and put them on a serving platter. Cover them with very damp paper towels. Thaw at room temperature for 1½ to 2 hours. Remove paper towels and serve.

TOAST CASES FOR HOT HORS-D'OEUVRE

These little cases are attractive and easy to prepare. When filled with a mixture and baked, they look as though a lot more work has gone into their preparation than really has.

With a 2¼-inch (5¾-centimeter) cutter, cut out bread rounds. Press them down into the cups of a muffin tin that has a diameter at

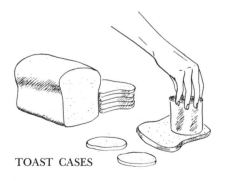

TOAST CASES

the base of 1¾ inches (4½ centimeters). If your cutters and muffin tins are not of these dimensions, then just cut the rounds a little larger than the diameter of the bottom of your muffin tin. Press them down on the bottom and against the side, making a raised edge about ¼ inch (¾ centimeter) high. Press the bread firmly.

You will get 2 rounds from each slice of bread. After you have cut the rounds, you can cut 2 rectangles from what is left over of each slice. *From 1 store loaf of white bread you can get 36 rounds and 36 rectangles.*

Bake in a 350° F. (180° C.) oven for 5 to 6 minutes. Just bake them long enough so that they feel dry to the touch but have not taken on any color. They will be fully baked later on with their filling. Cool the toast cases and pack in freezer bags. Make a lot of them, label, and store them in your freezer. These last a long time.

TOAST CASES FOR COLD HORS-D'OEUVRE

Follow the directions for Toast Cases for Hot Hors-d'Oeuvre but keep the muffin tins in the oven long enough for the cases to look nicely toasted as these will *not* be baked later on.

CROÛTES

These are small toast cases, easy and fun to make. You will need stale or dry bread, 2 sizes of cutters and some deep fat.

Buy an unsliced loaf of bread, or make some Juniper Hill Bread (see Index). Cut it into 1-inch (2½-centimeter) slices. Put the slices on a cooky sheet in one layer. Place in a 300° F. (150° C.) oven for 5 to 6 minutes. Cool uncovered.

Cut out 1½-inch (4-centimeter) rounds from the slices with a cooky or biscuit cutter. With a smaller cutter or a sharp knife, cut partway through the rounds in a little circle, leaving these circles in place. Fry a few at a time in deep fat heated to 370° F. (187° C.) for 30 seconds. They should be a deep golden color. Take them out with a slotted spoon and drain them on absorbent paper. With the point of a knife, pry up the center where you have scored it and scoop out a little hollow to contain whatever hors-d'oeuvre material you have chosen.

You can make these croûtes as large or small as you wish and in

CROÛTES

any shape that you like since they can be cut out with a knife as well as a cutter. Make a bunch of these and freeze them in freezer bags. When you take the croûtes out of the freezer, just pop them in a warm oven to thaw and dry them—3 to 4 minutes will do. Fill them with any of the cold hors-d'oeuvre material in this book.

You will get about 50 croûtes from a store loaf of bread and 60 to 70 from Juniper Hill Bread.

PATTY'S MELBA TOAST

1 loaf of unsliced white bread
½ pound (225 grams) unsalted butter

Cut the bread into ⅛-inch (½-centimeter) slices and remove the crusts. Cut in any desired shapes. Butter the slices and place them on a cooky sheet. Bake them in a very slow oven, 250° F. (120° C.), until they are dry and golden, 30 to 40 minutes.

Cool on a cake rack. Store in an airtight container or freeze them in freezer bags until needed.

When you want to use the frozen toasts, put them in a moderate oven for just a minute or two.

FLAKY PASTRY

1 cup (140 grams) unbleached flour
¼ teaspoon salt
1½ ounces (45 grams) butter
1 ounce (30 grams) lard
1 teaspoon lemon juice
¼ cup (½ deciliter) ice water

Put the flour and salt in a bowl. Cut the butter in slivers over the flour. Add the lard. Mix with the fingertips or pastry blender quickly and lightly, until the flour looks like little flakes. Put the lemon juice in the water and mix it quickly into the flour until the dough all comes together in one lump. Do not work the dough. Shape gently into a ball and wrap in plastic wrap. Chill in the refrigerator for 1 hour.

Roll out dough on a floured board ½ inch (1½ centimers) thick. Fold one third of the dough over the middle and the other third

over the double layer to make 3 layers. Now, fold the dough thus formed in half, pat down gently, and chill, wrapped in plastic wrap, for 1 hour. Roll out ⅛ inch (½ centimeter) thick and use as directed in the individual recipe.

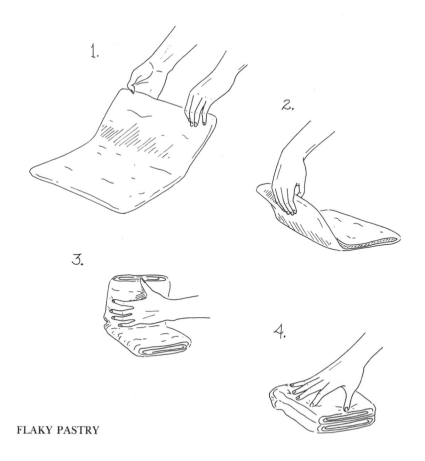

FLAKY PASTRY

PARTY CROUSTADES

PASTRY CROUSTADES

Make a double recipe of Flaky Pastry (preceding recipe). Roll out the pastry dough ¼ inch (¾ centimeter) thick. Cut out rounds with a 1¾-inch (4½-centimeter) cutter. Cut out the centers of half of them with a smaller cutter or a sharp knife. This will make a ¼-inch (¾-centimeter) ring of dough. Moisten the edges of the solid rounds with a little water and place a ring on top of each one. Bake on a cooky sheet in a 400° F. (205° C.) oven for 12 minutes. Cool. Freeze on a cooky sheet or whatever fits your freezer space. When frozen, put them carefully in freezer bags, label, and return to the freezer. *Makes about 34 croustades. Storage time: several months.*

To use: Remove the croustades from the freezer several hours before needed. Put them in a 300° F. (150° C.) oven for a few minutes to warm and dry out a little. Cool and fill with any cold hors-d'oeuvre mixture in this book.

NOTE: If you would like to serve *hot* croustades, bake the little pastry cases for only 5 minutes, until set. Freeze as above. When needed, remove the croustades from the freezer and fill with a *hot* hors-d'oeuvre mixture. Bake in a 400° F. (205° C.) oven for about 10 minutes.

TARTLET SHELLS FOR
HOT OR COLD HORS-D'OEUVRE

1½ cups (215 grams) unbleached flour
½ teaspoon baking powder
¼ teaspoon salt
4 ounces (115 grams) butter
2 egg yolks, slightly beaten
¼ teaspoon lemon juice
4 to 5 tablespoons (½ deciliter) ice water

Mix the dry ingredients in a bowl. Add the butter, cut into thin slivers. With the fingertips, rub ingredients together until the mixture resembles small flakes. Beat the egg yolks slightly and add to the dough along with the lemon juice and water. Use only as much of the water as you need. Still using the fingertips, mix the dough until it forms a ball. Wrap in plastic wrap and chill in the refrigerator for 1 hour.

Roll out the dough ⅛ inch (½ centimer) thick. With a cooky cutter, cut out rounds slightly larger than the bottom of the cups of an *inverted* muffin pan. Butter the bottoms. Place the rounds on the inverted cups and press them against the bottom and sides of the cups. This will make a tiny raised edge on the tartlet when it is baked. Put the inverted muffin pans on large cooky sheets.

If the tartlets will be served hot: Prick the bottoms with a fork and bake in a 375° F. (190° C.) oven for 4 minutes, until the pastry has set but has not taken on any color. Cool slightly and lift off. When cold, fill with whatever hot hors-d'oeuvre filling you have chosen. Freeze on a cooky sheet or whatever fits your freezer space. When frozen, put the filled tartlets in freezer bags, label, and return to the freezer. *Makes about 36 tartlets. Storage time: whatever time is given for the individual filling material.*

To use: Bake in a 400° F. (205° C.) oven for 6 to 8 minutes, or until the pastry is golden and the filling is hot and bubbly.

If the tartlets are to be served cold: Prepare them as for hot tartlets, only bake the shells longer—6 to 8 minutes, or until golden. Cool. Fill the tartlets with whatever *cold* hors-d'oeuvre material you have chosen. Freeze the same as for the hot tartlets.

To use: Arrange the frozen tartlets on a serving platter. Cover with *dry* paper towels and thaw at room temperature for 2 hours. Remove towels and serve.

PASTRY PUFFS
(Petits Choux)

    1 cup (140 grams) unbleached flour
    1 cup (¼ liter) water
    4 ounces (115 grams) butter
    ¼ teaspoon salt
    1 tablespoon grated Parmesan cheese
    4 eggs

Sift the flour before measuring. Heat water, butter and salt together. When butter melts and water is boiling, remove from heat and add the flour all at once. Return to the heat and stir until dough forms a ball and leaves the side of the pan. Remove the mixture from the heat and add the cheese. Beat well. Add eggs, one at a time, beating well after each additon. Drop by level teaspoons onto a buttered baking sheet, keeping them 1 inch (2½ centimeters) apart. Bake in a 400° F. (205° C.) oven for 10 minutes. Reduce heat to 350° F. (180° C.) and cook for another 20 minutes. They should be about 1¾ inches (4½ centimeters) across when cooked. Remove from oven and cool. Put the puffs in freezer bags, label, and freeze. *Makes about 60 tiny cream puffs. Storage time: several months.*

To use: Several hours before needed, remove the pastry puffs from the freezer and place on a cooky sheet. Bake in 300° F. (150° C.) oven for 5 to 6 minutes to warm and dry out. Cool.

To fill: Meantime, defrost the containers of filling as described in the individual recipes. The filling needs to be removed from freezer earlier than the puffs. There are two ways to fill the puffs:

1. Put the filling mixture in a pastry bag or tube and use a tip with a large opening. Insert the point of a knife in the side of the puff near the bottom. Put the tip of the pastry bag or tube in the opening and squeeze about 1 generous teaspoon of the filling into the tiny puff. Gently close the hole with your fingers and set aside. Do the others the same way.

2. Slice the bottom of a pastry puff three quarters of the way through, leaving a kind of hinge. Spoon the filling into the puff. Close the bottom and gently press the two parts together. The filling will help to stick them together.

NOTE: These pastry puffs may be frozen already filled. They are good this way, too, but the puffs are not as crispy as they are when re-warmed before filling.

Once you have a batch of these little puffs made and in the freezer you can fill them with many of the cold canapé spreads given in this book. They are great to have on hand if you see a party coming in the not too distant future.

BLUE-CHEESE PASTRY I

1 cup (140 grams) unbleached flour
¼ teaspoon salt
2 ounces (60 grams) blue cheese
2 ounces (60 grams) cream cheese
4 ounces (115 grams) butter

Sift the flour and salt into a bowl. Cut thin slivers of both cheeses and the butter on top of the flour. Work them into the flour with the fingertips. When well blended, shape into a ball. Flatten the ball and wrap in wax paper. Chill in the refrigerator for 1 hour. Roll out as directed in the individual recipe.

BLUE-CHEESE PASTRY II

2 cups (285 grams) sifted unbleached flour
4 ounces (115 grams) blue cheese
½ teaspoon salt
4 ounces (115 grams) butter
5 to 6 tablespoons (½ deciliter) very cold water

Sift the flour into a bowl. Grate the blue cheese over it. Add the salt and cut the butter in slivers over the flour and cheese. Mix quickly with the fingertips or pastry blender until thoroughly mixed. Add water, only as much as needed, and mix carefully, without too much handling, until dough forms a ball. Wrap the ball in wax paper and chill for 1 hour. Roll out as directed in the individual recipe.

PATTY SHELLS

2 cups (285 grams) sifted flour
½ teaspoon salt
6 ounces (180 grams) butter
2 ounces (60 grams) lard
5 tablespoons (½ deciliter) ice water

Mix the flour and salt together and cut in the butter and lard with a pastry blender, or mix lightly and quickly with the fingertips, until the dough is in pea-size lumps. Add the water and mix quickly with a fork or the fingertips until it all holds together. The dough will be somewhat sticky. Wrap in wax paper and chill for 1 hour.

Roll out on a well-floured surface into an oblong shape ¼ inch (¾ centimeter) thick. Fold one end toward the middle and fold the other end over on top of it. Again roll out ¼ inch thick and cut out rounds with a 1½-inch (4-centimeter) cutter. Cut the centers out of half of the rounds with a smaller cutter or glass, leaving a ¼-inch (¾-centimeter) ring of dough. Dampen the edges of the larger solid rounds and place the rings on top. Press them down gently. Fill the centers with a tiny amount of any of the recipes for hot hors-d'oeuvre. Take the rest of the leftover pieces and roll them together. Fold in thirds as before and chill again for 30 minutes. Roll out and cut out a few more rounds. *Makes about 24 pastries.* Freeze on a cooky sheet or whatever fits into your freezer space. When frozen, put in freezer bags, label, and return to the freezer. *Storage time: 1 month.*

To use: Bake the frozen shells in a 400° F. (205° C.) oven for about 15 minutes, or until the sides of the patty shell have risen high around the filling and are golden and puffy. Serve hot.

NOTE: These patty shells may be made and baked without the filling. Freeze them in freezer bags. Thaw at room temperature when needed and fill with your favorite cold hors-d'oeuvre mixture.

To Use Recipes as Spreads or Dips

Most of the cold mixtures in this book may be used as a spread or dip. The big advantage to this is that you may freeze a mixture in a freezer container and, when thawed, it can be spread on crackers at the cocktail table. If it is thinned out with a little sweet or sour cream it can be used as a dip.

As a spread: Prepare one of the recipes and put it in a freezer container of the appropriate size for that particular recipe. Freeze it and store it for the recommended time.

To use: Thaw in the freezer container in the refrigerator for 24 hours. An hour or so before the cocktail hour, whip mixture with a wire whisk or fork. Put it on a serving platter and shape it any way you wish. Decorate it with parsley, nuts or whatever seems most appropriate for that particular dish.

As a dip: When thawed, whip mixture with a wire whisk or fork, adding a bit of sweet or sour cream to the recipe until it is soft enough to serve as a dip for vegetable slices, potato chips, toast or crackers. Don't thin it too much or it won't stay on the things your guests are dipping into it.

Garnishes

Anchovies are included in many of my recipes because I like the salty flavor. If they are too salty for your taste, put them in a strainer and run cold water over them; then dry them in paper towels before using them in a recipe. Or, if you do not share my enthusiasm for them, make substitutions where needed: use celery salt, seasoned salt, smoky salt or other seasonings.

Cream cheese is basic. It freezes well, keeps well, and is just about foolproof.

Parsley when used as a garnish must be handled with great care. After it is frozen it becomes very brittle, so don't just dump the parsley-decorated canapés into the freezer bags—easy does it! Once thawed under the paper towels, parsley becomes soft again. This is true of celery tops, watercress and other green garnishes also. Only use a tiny piece of a green for garnish as a large piece looks limp on the thawed canapé. It is only a matter of a moment or two if you wish to garnish your canapés after they are thawed instead of freezing them with the garnish in place. Garnishes can be frozen on the canapé, but if you choose to do it later, you will find it easier getting hors-d'oeuvre in and out of the bags without worrying about breaking off the parsley or watercress. However, if great care is taken, it can be done.

Grated hard-cooked egg yolks are a pretty garnish and freeze well. Grate them and spoon them into 1-pint (½-liter) bags, 2 egg yolks per bag. Package them loosely, seal, and freeze. When frozen, the small packages can be put in a larger one so they don't get lost in the freezer. Label the larger bag. Thaw them (as many as you need) in the refrigerator overnight. Separate the pieces lightly with a fork and sprinkle on the canapés.

Some canapés will be garnished with things like capers or caviar. Handle these carefully, too, so they won't be knocked off while being transferred to the freezer bag.

TOASTED ALMONDS

Preheat oven to 400° F. (205° C.). Put blanched almonds, whole, slivered or sliced, in a single layer on a cooky sheet and place them in the oven. Stirring and checking them constantly, allow the almonds to become golden brown. If you take your eyes off of them for more than a minute they will burn, so watch carefully. The aroma which wafts from the oven will tell you a lot. When they are exactly ready and start to "crackle," the smell is heavenly and you'll find that the nose knows that they are done.

TOASTED COCONUT

Put the contents of a 7-ounce (200-gram) package of coconut on a cooky sheet and place it in a 400° F. (205° C.) oven. Watch it very carefully and stir it around occasionally until it becomes an even golden brown. Remove from the oven and let it cool off the hot pan for 5 minutes before using.

This may also be prepared in the small pan of a toaster-oven, set at "top brown," or under the broiler. In every case, watch constantly

as it only takes a few minutes and will brown too much if you turn
your back on it.

BRANDIED RAISINS

Empty the contents of a 10-ounce (283.5-gram) box of raisins, black
or white, into a glass jar with a lid. Pour in brandy to cover, and put
the lid on the jar. Cover tightly and store in a dark place. Shake
them up once in a while. It takes about a month for them to puff up
and be ready to use. I keep a jar of them on hand at all times as they
are wonderful in hors-d'oeuvre and on or in ice cream. As they are
used, just keep adding more raisins and shake them up.

CHEESES

It's hard to beat a beautiful, just-ripe Brie, a creamy blue or soft Camembert surrounded with crisp crackers, but there are ways to glorify these already tasty cheeses to make them delectable in a different way.

A canned freestone peach, for instance, bears no resemblance whatever to a tree-ripe peach but it is delicious just the same. This is also true of canned artichoke hearts or asparagus but there are many ways we use and enjoy them in our cooking.

One of my favorite cheeses is Camembert. Even though I love it just as it is, I decided to experiment with it. One dark March day I came up with curried Camembert, which has turned out to be a popular variation of an already delightful cheese. It is easy and quick to whip up at a moment's notice and freezes well. It is also one of the hors-d'oeuvre that lasts the longest in the freezer. Another delicious combination is Brie and toasted almonds. Both recipes are in this book.

You can keep a large supply of good Cheddar, Parmesan or Swiss cheese in the freezer at all times. Grate it and put it in labeled quart (liter) bags. Then it is always ready for use. Use as much as a recipe calls for and put the rest back in the freezer. It keeps almost indefinitely.

Packaged cream cheese may be frozen, also, for use in my recipes. It tends to crumble when thawed, but when mashed and added to other ingredients, it pulls itself together again and looks and tastes as good as new.

The Gouda and Edam round cheeses are delicious plain, or you can hollow them out and stuff them; very festive and unusual they are, too. There are recipes here for their preparation.

There are so many wonderful cheeses in this world and so many excellent books on the subject that I shan't dwell on them here. It just seems to me that cheeses offer one of the most creative areas for experimentation in taste. Take some of your favorite flavors and mix them with your favorite cheeses and see what comes of it. Maybe disaster, and you feed it to the cat. On the other hand, and far more likely, maybe it will be the discovery of the best canapé material you ever tasted.

HOT CHEESE AND GINGER CANAPÉS

1 loaf of white bread
5 ounces (140 grams) Cheddar cheese, grated
2 ounces (60 grams) cream cheese
½ teaspoon ground ginger
1 tablespoon sherry
ground black pepper
¼ teaspoon paprika

Remove crusts from the bread slices and cut the slices into rectangles. There are 6 rectangles in 1 slice of store bread. Put them on a cooky sheet and into a 350° F. (180° C.) oven for 5 to 6 minutes. Bake them until they are just dry to the touch. They should not take on any color as they will be baked later on. Remove them and cover with a dry towel.

Mash the Cheddar cheese and the cream cheese together. Add all other ingredients, with black pepper to taste, and mix well. Mound on the toast rectangles. Place canapés on a cooky sheet or whatever fits your freezer space and put in the freezer. When frozen, put the canapés in freezer bags, label, and return to the freezer. *Makes about 25 canapés. Storage time: 1 month.*

To use: Put the frozen hors-d'oeuvre on a broiler pan and broil for 2 to 3 minutes, or until they are heated through, puffy and slightly brown. Serve hot with plenty of napkins.

BLUE CHEESE ANCHOVY CANAPÉS

1 loaf of rye bread
1 ounce (30 grams) butter for rounds (⅛ teaspoon per round)
4 ounces (115 grams) whole pimientos
4 ounces (115 grams) blue cheese
3 ounces (90 grams) cream cheese
cream
4 ounces (115 grams) rolled anchovy fillets

Cut 1½-inch (4-centimeter) rounds out of the rye bread slices. Butter them.

Drain and dry the pimientos, cut into thin strips, and set aside. Mash both cheeses together and add enough cream to make a soft paste. Spread on the prepared rounds. Place a rolled anchovy fillet on top and wrap a strip of pimiento around it. Press gently to secure it.

Freeze the canapés on a cooky sheet or whatever fits your freezer space. When frozen, put the canapés in freezer bags, label, and return to the freezer. *Makes about 30 canapés. Storage time: 3 weeks.*

To use: Remove canapés carefully from their bags. Arrange them on a serving platter and cover with very damp paper towels. Thaw at room temperature for 1½ to 2 hours. Remove paper towels and serve.

PUMPERNICKEL CHEESE ROUNDS

1 large loaf of pumpernickel bread
2 ounces (60 grams) butter for rounds (⅛ teaspoon per round)
4 ounces (115 grams) blue cheese
4 ounces (115 grams) cream cheese
1 ounce (30 milliliters) sherry
½ teaspoon ground rosemary
1 tablespoon minced parsley
salt and ground pepper
5½ ounces (160 grams) slivered blanched almonds, chopped

The spread alone can be frozen in 1-quart (1-liter) freezer containers to be spread on the rounds another day.

Cut 1½-inch (4-centimeter) rounds out of the pumpernickel bread with a cooky cutter. Butter them.

Mix all ingredients except the almonds together, and heap on the pumpernickel rounds. Spread out the chopped almonds on a flat surface and turn each of the bread rounds over on the nuts. Press gently so that the almonds will adhere to the mixture. Freeze on a cooky sheet or whatever fits your freezer space. When frozen, put the canapés in freezer bags, label, and return to the freezer. *Makes 50 canapés. Storage time: 1 month or more.*

To use: Remove canapés carefully from the freezer and put them on a serving platter. Cover them with very damp paper towels. Thaw at room temperature for 1½ to 2 hours. Remove paper towels and serve.

To freeze in a container: Mix the spread and mix the chopped slivered almonds right into the spread. Pack into a 1-quart (1-liter) freezer container, label, and freeze.

To use: Thaw the container of spread in the refrigerator for 24 hours. Place the spread on a serving platter and shape it into a flattened ball. Decorate with some fresh parsley. *Serves about 10 people.*

CURRIED CAMEMBERT CANAPÉS

1 loaf of white bread
1½ ounces (45 grams) butter for rounds (⅛ teaspoon per round)
4 ounces (115 grams) Camembert cheese
2¾ ounces (78 grams) whole blanched almonds
⅓ teaspoon grated onion
2 ounces (60 grams) cream cheese
2 tablespoons (30 milliliters) dairy sour cream
½ teaspoon curry powder

Cut out the bread rounds with a 1½-inch (4-centimeter) cutter, or any shape you wish. Butter them.

Mash the Camembert with a fork or put it through the round holes of a cheese grater.

Toast the almonds in a preheated 400° F. (205° C.) oven. Watch them carefully so that they just look golden-amber colored, not any darker or they get bitter.

Add grated onion to the Camembert. Mash the cream cheese and add it, sour cream and curry powder to the Camembert and onion. Mix well.

Spread the mixture on the prepared buttered bread rounds. Top each canapé with a whole toasted almond. Freeze the canapés on a cooky sheet or whatever fits your freezer space. When frozen, put the canapés in freezer bags, label, and return to the freezer. *Makes about 35 canapés. Storage time: 3 weeks.*

To use: Take canapés from the freezer and arrange them on a serving platter. Cover them with very damp paper towels. Thaw at room temperature for 1½ to 2 hours. Remove paper towels and serve.

These canapés actually improve with storage for 1 to 2 weeks. The curry seems to mellow and blend in better with the Camembert.

As a spread: Freeze in 1-quart (1-liter) freezer containers; label. Freeze the almonds also.

To use: Thaw the spread and the almonds in the refrigerator for 24 hours. Whip the spread with a fork or wire whisk and place on a serving platter. Shape in a ball, log or whatever, and decorate with the defrosted almonds.

HOT CHEDDAR CANAPÉS

1 large loaf of rye bread
4 ounces (115 grams) Cheddar cheese, grated
2 teaspoons prepared mustard
1 tablespoon chili sauce
2 teaspoons paprika
1 tablespoon sherry
pinch of dried tarragon

Cut out the bread rounds with a 1¾-inch (4½-centimeter) round cooky cutter or make them any other shape you wish. Put them on a cooky sheet and into a preheated oven set at 350° F. (180° C.). Leave them for 5 to 6 minutes. They should be a little dry to the touch but should not take on any color as they will be broiled later on. Remove the rounds, cover them with a dry towel, and allow to cool.

Mix the remaining ingredients together by mashing them well with a fork. Spread not too thickly on the cooled rye toast rounds. Freeze on a cooky sheet or whatever fits your freezer space. When frozen, put the canapés in freezer bags, label, and return to the freezer. *Makes 50 canapés. Storage time: 1 month.*

To use: Put the frozen canapés in the broiler 4 to 6 inches (10 to 15 centimeters) from the source of heat. Broil until puffy and golden.

BRIE CHEESE WITH TOASTED ALMONDS

2¾ ounces (78 grams) slivered blanched almonds
1 loaf of white bread
1 ounce (30 grams) butter for the rounds (⅛ teaspoon per
     round)
8 ounces (225 grams) Brie cheese
dairy sour cream

Preheat oven to 400° F. (205° C.). Put the slivered almonds on a
cooky sheet and place them in the oven. Watch them carefully so
that they do not burn. You want them a golden-amber color. Remove from oven and cool.

With a cooky cutter, cut out 1½-inch (4-centimeter) rounds of
white bread. Butter them.

Mash the cheese with a fork, or, if it is not too soft, put it
through the round holes of a cheese grater. Chop the cooled nuts,
having reserved about 30 almond slivers for decorating. Add the
chopped nuts to the cheese and add enough sour cream (very little)
to make it of spreading consistency. Heap the mixture on the prepared bread rounds and place a slivered almond on top.

Freeze on a cooky sheet or whatever fits your freezer space.
When frozen, put the canapés in freezer bags, label, and return to
the freezer. *Makes about 30 canapés. Storage time: 3 weeks.*

To use: Take from the freezer and remove carefully from the
bags. Place the frozen hors-d'oeuvre on a serving platter and cover
with very damp paper towels. Thaw at room temperature for 1½ to
2 hours. Remove paper towels and serve.

STUFFED CHEESE

1 large Edam or Gouda cheese, about 2 pounds (.9 kilogram)
4 ounces (115 grams) cream cheese
4 ounces (115 grams) butter
2 tablespoons (30 milliliters) yogurt
2 ounces (½ deciliter) white port or white rum
1 teaspoon caraway seeds (optional)

With a sharp knife cut the top off the round cheese about one fifth of the way down. To be very fancy, you can plunge the knife in at that spot and instead of a smooth cut, make a zigzag pattern like the teeth of a jack-o'-lantern, as shown in the drawing.

Scoop out the inside of the cheese, being very careful not to remove any of the wax on the outside; leave the shell intact. Put this cheese through the finest blade of a meat grinder. Mash the cream cheese, butter and yogurt together and add the cheese that you have scooped out. Mash everything together until no lumps remain. Add the white port or rum, and the caraway seeds if used. Mix stuffing thoroughly and put back into the shell as much as will fit and still be able to put the top back on. Put any that is left over in a freezer container to use another day.

Wrap the cheese (with its top on) in freezer paper, seal it with freezer tape, label, and freeze. *Storage time: 1 month.*

To use: Thaw, still wrapped, in the refrigerator for at least 24 hours, then at room temperature for 4 to 6 hours. Unwrap, remove the top, and fluff up the cheese with a fork, adding a little more port, if necessary. Serve surrounded with crackers. *Serves 10 to 15 people.*

NOTE: If your market does not carry these large cheeses, look for the small cheeses, 12 to 16 ounces (336 to 453 grams). Stuff two of the small ones. There are also much larger cheeses, 3½ to 4 pounds (1.6 to 1.8 kilograms). If you have one of these, double all the other ingredients for the stuffing.

VARIATION:
STUFFED CHEESE WITH PICKLED ONIONS

    1 large Edam or Gouda cheese
    4 ounces (115 grams) cream cheese
    4 ounces (115 grams) butter
    ½ teaspoon curry powder
    12 sweet pickled onions, minced

Prepare the Gouda or Edam shell as in the basic recipe. Mix all ingredients and stuff and freeze the same way. The sweet little onions give an unusual flavor to the cheese. *Storage time: 1 month.*

JUNIPER HILL'S CHEESE SPREAD
AND CANAPÉS

1 large loaf of pumpernickel bread
2 to 2½ ounces (60 to 75 grams) soft butter for the rounds (⅛
    teaspoon per round)
6 ounces (180 grams) cream cheese
2 ounces (60 grams) cottage cheese
¼ cup (½ deciliter) grated Cheddar cheese
2 ounces (60 grams) butter
1 teaspoon chopped capers
1 teaspoon caraway seeds
1 teaspoon paprika
4 anchovy fillets, minced
3 tablespoons (45 milliliters) flat beer
2 tablespoons (30 milliliters) mayonnaise
1 onion, minced
60 whole capers for garnish

Cut the bread rounds with a 1½-inch (4-centimeter) cutter or
any shape you wish. Butter them.

Work cheeses and 2 ounces butter together until smooth. Add
remaining ingredients except the 60 whole capers, and mix
thoroughly. Spread on prepared bread rounds. Top each with a
whole caper. Freeze the canapés on a cooky sheet or whatever fits
your freezer space. When frozen, put the canapés in freezer bags,
label, and return to the freezer. *Makes about 60 canapés. Storage time:
3 weeks.*

To use: Take from the freezer and remove canapés carefully
from the bags. Place them on a serving platter and cover with very
damp paper towels. Thaw at room temperature for 1½ to 2 hours.
Remove paper towels and serve.

As a spread: Make the recipe as described, omitting the 60
whole capers. Put spread in a 1-quart (1-liter) container, label, and
freeze. *This will serve about 10 people. Storage time: 1 month.*

To use: Thaw in the refrigerator for 24 hours. Whip the spread
with a fork or wire whisk. On a serving platter, shape it into a log or
whatever shape you can dream up. Surround with crackers or Melba
toast. Decorate with watercress sprigs or fresh parsley and capers.

ALMOND CREAM-CHEESE CANAPÉS

1 loaf of white bread
1½ ounces (45 grams) soft butter for the bread rounds (⅛ teaspoon per round)
5½ ounces (160 grams) slivered blanched almonds
4 ounces (115 grams) cream cheese, softened
4 ounces (115 grams) butter
⅓ orange, grated rind and juice
1 ounce (30 milliliters) wild cherry brandy, kirsch or rum
salt

Cut the bread rounds with a 1½-inch (4-centimeter) cutter or any shape you wish. Butter them.

Toast the almonds in a 400° F. (205° C.) oven until they are a very light brown. Do not let them get too dark. When they are cool, coarsely chop half of them.

Mash the cheese and butter and mix well. Add the *chopped* almonds to the cheese. Add all other ingredients except the unchopped almonds. Use salt to taste. Mix together well and spread thickly on the prepared bread rounds. Top each canapé with a slivered almond. Press down gently.

Freeze canapés on a cooky sheet or whatever fits your freezer space. When frozen, put them in freezer bags, label, and return to the freezer. *Makes about 50 canapés. Storage time: 3 weeks.*

To use: Take canapés from the freezer and remove carefully from the bags. Place them on a serving platter and cover with very damp paper towels. Thaw at room temperature for 1½ to 2 hours. Remove paper towels and serve.

ALMOND BLUE-CHEESE CANAPÉS

1 loaf of wheat or oatmeal bread
1 to 1½ ounces (30 to 45 grams) butter for rounds (⅛ teaspoon
    per round)
2¾ ounces (78 grams) slivered blanched almonds
4 ounces (115 grams) blue cheese
4 ounces (115 grams) cream cheese
2 ounces (60 grams) butter, softened
2 tablespoons (30 milliliters) minced chutney
2 teaspoons Worcestershire sauce
1 tablespoon chopped parsley
salt

Cut out the bread rounds with a 1½-inch (4-centimeter) cutter
or any shape you wish. Butter them.

Toast the almonds in a 400° F. (205° C.) oven until they are a
light brown. Chop them coarsely.

Mash cheeses and 2 ounces butter together. Add half of the
chopped almonds and all other ingredients to the mixture. Use salt
to taste. Heap on the prepared bread rounds. Sprinkle remaining almonds on top. Press down gently. Freeze on a cooky sheet or whatever fits your freezer space. When frozen, put the canapés in freezer
bags, label, and return to freezer. *Makes about 40 canapés. Storage
time: 3 weeks.*

To use: Take from the freezer and remove canapés carefully
from the bags. Place them on a serving platter and cover with very
damp paper towels. Thaw at room temperature for 1½ to 2 hours.
Remove paper towels and serve.

JUNIPER HILL CHEESE BALL

8 ounces (225 grams) cream cheese
2 ounces (60 grams) blue cheese
4 ounces (113 grams) whole pimientos
2¾ ounces (78 grams) slivered or sliced blanched almonds
2 ounces (60 grams) butter, softened
1 teaspoon grated onion
3 tablespoons (45 milliliters) minced dill pickle
2 tablespoons (30 milliliters) mayonnaise
1 teaspoon soy sauce
1 tablespoon paprika

Mash both cheeses. Cut 2 whole pimientos into halves and dry them thoroughly with paper towels. Mince them. Put the almonds in the blender and pulverize them. Mix all ingredients together and taste for seasoning. Put in a 1-quart (1-liter) freezer container, label, and freeze. *Serves 10 to 12 people. Storage time: several months.*

To use: Thaw in the container in the refrigerator for 24 hours. Put the mixture in a bowl and whip it up with a fork or wire whisk. Shape into a ball and put on a serving platter. Decorate with pretty greens and serve with rye crackers.

DEVILED CHEESE CANAPÉS

2¾ ounces (78 grams) slivered blanched almonds
1 large loaf of pumpernickel bread
1 ounce (30 grams) butter for the rounds (⅛ teaspoon per
    round)
3 ounces (90 grams) cream cheese
1 ounce (30 grams) butter
1 green pepper
3 pitted black olives
2 tablespoons (30 milliliters) mayonnaise
2 teaspoons pickle relish
2 teaspoons chili sauce
½ teaspoon prepared Dijon mustard
½ teaspoon onion salt
ground pepper

The spread alone can be frozen in a 1-quart (1-liter) freezer container to be spread on rounds another day.

Preheat oven to 400° F. (205° C.). Put the slivered almonds on a cooky sheet and into the oven. Watch them carefully so they do not burn. You want them a golden-amber color. Remove from the oven and cool. Pulverize the almonds in a blender. Set aside.

Cut out the pumpernickel rounds with a 1½-inch (4-centimeter) cutter, or any shape you wish. Butter them.

Mash the cream cheese and 1 ounce butter together. Finely mince 1 tablespoon of green pepper and the 3 olives. Add them and all other ingredients, including the ground almonds, to the cheese mixture. Use black pepper to taste. Heap the mixture on the rounds and decorate each one with a thin sliver of green pepper. Press down gently. Place on a cooky sheet or whatever fits into your freezer space. When frozen, put the canapés in freezer bags, label, and return to the freezer. *Makes about 30 canapés. Storage time: 1 month.*

To use: Take from the freezer and remove canapés carefully from the bags. Place them on a serving platter and cover with very damp paper towels. Thaw at room temperature for 1½ to 2 hours. Remove paper towels and serve.

To freeze in a container: Mix the spread as directed in the recipe and put it in a 1-quart (1-liter) freezer container, label, and freeze.

To use: Remove spread from the freezer 24 hours before needed and thaw in the refrigerator. Put the spread on a serving platter and shape it into any shape you wish. Decorate with fresh parsley or a few pieces of green pepper slivers. *Serves 6 to 8 people.*

BLACK-OLIVE CHEESE ROLL

8 ounces (225 grams) cream cheese
1 ounce (30 grams) blue cheese
4 ounces (115 grams) butter
¼ cup (½ deciliter) minced celery
¼ cup (½ deciliter) minced green pepper
8 pitted black olives, minced
2 tablespoons minced parsley
2 teaspoons soy sauce
1 tablespoon mayonnaise
garlic powder and ground pepper
paprika
celery leaves
cocktail crackers (your choice)

Mash the cheeses with a fork. Add the butter and mix well. Add the vegetables and olives with the soy sauce, mayonnaise, and garlic powder and pepper to taste to the cheese mixture. Mix thoroughly. Spoon into a 1-quart (1-liter) freezer container, Label and freeze. *Serves 10 to 15 people. Storage time: 2 months.*

To use: Thaw in the refrigerator for 24 hours. Whip the mixture with a fork or wire whisk and shape it on a serving platter into a log or roll. Score the top of the roll with the tines of a fork and sprinkle with paprika. Surround with celery heart leaves. Serve with crackers.

CHEESE PUFFS WITH BLUE-CHEESE CREAM

4 ounces (115 grams) blue cheese
8 ounces (225 grams) cream cheese
2 teaspoons grated onion
2 ounces (60 milliliters) sherry, port or Madeira
1 recipe Pastry Puffs (see Index)

Mash the cheeses and add other filling ingredients. Mix well and put in 1-pint (½-liter) freezer containers, label, and freeze.

To use: Remove the containers from the freezer to refrigerator for 24 hours before needed.

Several hours before you are ready to fill the puffs, remove them from freezer, re-warm them, and cool them as described in that recipe.

Whip the blue-cheese cream and fill the puffs, using whichever method is easier for you. *Makes about 60 puffs.*

CHEESE WAFERS

8 ounces (225 grams) Cheddar or blue cheese
4 ounces (115 grams) butter
1 cup (140 grams) unbleached flour
¼ teaspoon salt
½ teaspoon paprika, extra for garnish

Grate the cheese and mix it well with the butter. Add all other ingredients and blend thoroughly. Shape in a long roll 1½ inches (4 centimeters) thick. Chill. With a sharp knife cut the roll into ¼-inch (¾-centimeter) thick slices. Put slices on a cooky sheet or whatever fits your freezer space. Dust the wafers with the additional paprika and freeze. When frozen, put in freezer bags, label, and return to the freezer. *Makes about 4 dozen wafers. Storage time: several months.*

To use: Pop the frozen cheese wafers into a 400° F. (205° C.) oven on an *un*buttered cooky sheet for about 5 to 6 minutes, or until puffy and golden.

CHEDDAR TWISTS

2 cups (285 grams) unbleached flour
¼ teaspoon salt
4 ounces (115 grams) Cheddar cheese, grated
4 ounces (115 grams) butter
1 teaspoon paprika
6 tablespoons cream or water
1 tablespoon sesame seeds

Put the flour and salt in a bowl. Grate the cheese over and slice the butter on top. Add the paprika. With the fingertips or a pastry blender, mix together. Add cream or water and stir until the dough is well mixed. Form into a ball and wrap in plastic wrap. Chill in the refrigerator for 1 hour.

Roll the dough out on a floured board ¼ inch (¾ centimeter) thick. Sprinkle with sesame seeds and roll them in gently with the rolling pin. With a sharp knife or pastry wheel, cut into strips ½ inch (1½ centimeters) wide and about 8 inches (20 centimeters) long. Twist strips to make spirals. Put them on a cooky sheet or whatever fits your freezer space. When frozen, put them in freezer bags, label, and return to the freezer. *Makes about 30 Cheddar twists. Storage time: several months.*

To use: Bake the frozen twists on a cooky sheet in a 350° F. (180° C.) oven for 15 minutes. They should be deep gold in color and very crispy. Serve warm or cold.

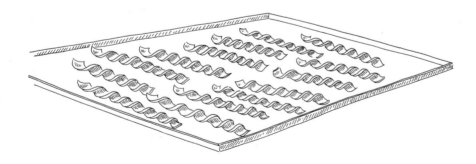

CHEESE ALMOND CRISPIES

4 ounces (115 grams) Cheddar cheese, grated
2 ounces (60 grams) butter
½ cup (70 grams) unbleached flour
⅛ teaspoon salt
¼ teaspoon paprika, or more
1 egg mixed with 1 teaspoon water
2¾ ounces (78 grams) slivered blanched almonds

Cream the cheese and butter together. Add flour, salt and paprika. Mix well and form into a ball. Wrap in wax paper and chill in the refrigerator for 1 hour. Roll out the dough ⅛ inch (½ centimeter) thick. With a sharp knife or pastry wheel, cut diagonally two ways to make diamond shapes. Mix the egg with the water and brush the pastry with it. Sprinkle a little additional paprika on the diamonds and then put on the almonds. Press them down gently to secure them. Bake in a preheated 375° F. (190° C.) oven for 8 to 10 minutes, until lightly browned. Cool and put into 1-quart (1-liter) freezer bags. Handle them carefully so that the almonds will stay in place. Label and freeze. *Makes about 36 diamonds, depending on your cutting expertise.*

To use: Put the diamond-shaped wafers on a cooky sheet and cover with a dry towel. Allow to thaw at room temperature. If desired, they can be put in a warm oven for a few minutes before serving.

FISH AND SHELLFISH

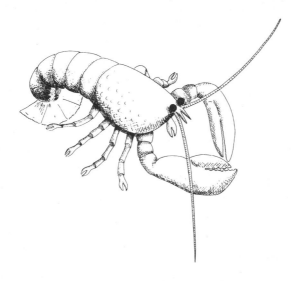

My love affair with the sea began at the age of ten when I was taken with a boatload of grown-ups on a deep-sea fishing expedition off the Isles of Shoals, New Hampshire. It was a memorable experience for me, made more so by my winning $2.75 for catching the biggest fish! It seemed a monster. It was a rock cod and weighed 22 pounds. I tipped the scales at only 85 pounds so the struggle was a mighty one.

Here in Maine, some of the men who catch the fish sell their own fresh-caught fish in trucks and stands by the roadside. Most of them have their own boats so can guarantee the freshness of the product they sell.

When not using fresh seafood, the canned variety is quite acceptable, and I wouldn't be caught without a good supply. I recommend keeping at least one can each of oysters, clams, smoked mussels, salmon and crab meat on hand at all times. If you haven't stuffed your freezer with already prepared hors-d'oeuvre, you can make them up in a jiffy by using some cream cheese, or butter, or yogurt, or sour cream. Add a few fine herbs, fresh or dried, and some spices and you will be all set for surprise company. The purpose of this book, however, is to help you have *prepared* hors-d'oeuvre in the freezer for that kind of company. A bag full of crab-meat canapés or salmon pinwheels would save the day and really surprise that surprise guest. Fifteen minutes from freezer to oven to platter—that's the way to do it!

ANCHOVIES IN BLUE-CHEESE PASTRY

Blue-Cheese Pastry I (see Index)
1 ounce (30 grams) flat anchovy fillets
4 ounces (115 grams) cream cheese
grated rind of ½ lemon
1 tablespoon mayonnaise
1 teaspoon prepared mustard
1 egg mixed with 2 teaspoons water

Mix the pastry, shape it into 2 equal-size balls, flatten them, and chill in the refrigerator for 30 minutes. Roll each ball into a rectangular shape roughly 7 × 10 inches (18 × 25 centimeters) and ⅛ inch (½ centimeter) thick.

Drain, dry, and mince the anchovies. Mash the cheese with a fork and add the anchovies, lemon rind, mayonnaise and mustard. Mix them well into a smooth paste. Spread on one of the rolled-out pastry rectangles. Cover with the other pastry rectangle, easing it to fit. Roll again, lightly, to enlarge the dough a bit and to secure the filling (never mind if some of the filling runs out). Place between 2 sheets of wax paper (to keep out the air) and chill in the refrigerator for 30 minutes. Put the pastry on a lightly floured board. With a pastry wheel or sharp knife, cut into strips 1¾ inches (4½ centimeters) the long way, then into strips 1½ inches (4 centimeters) at right angles to the first cut. You will have small rectangular filled pastries. Place them on a cooky sheet or whatever fits your freezer space. Mix the egg and water and brush the tops of the pastries with it. Freeze. When frozen, put the anchovy-filled pastries in freezer bags, label, and return to the freezer. *Makes about 40 pastries. Storage time: 1 month.*

NOTE: Obviously, it will not be possible to make the 2 balls exactly the same size, or to roll them out so they will exactly fit each other. So here's what you do: After rolling, filling, and stacking the layers one on top of the other, trim off all the scraggly edges, making a neat rectangle. Then cut out the filled pastries as explained in the recipe and put them on the cooky sheet. Gather up all the leftovers. With flour on your fingers, roll this leftover anchovy pastry into a single ball in the palms of your hands. On a well-floured board, roll the ball out as you did before. You will need to flour the rolling pin and keep turning the pastry over to keep it from sticking. With your pastry wheel or knife, cut the pastry into thin strips about ⅓ inch (1 centimeter) wide and as long as you wish. Freeze as instructed.

To use: Place the frozen pastries and/or the thin strips in a 400° F. (205° C.) oven; allow 6 minutes for the strips and 9 minutes for the pastries. The little strips make very good cocktail "nibbles."

ANCHOVY CAPER CANAPÉS

1 loaf of pumpernickel bread
1½ ounces (45 grams) soft butter for the rounds (⅛ teaspoon per round)
1 ounce (30 grams) flat anchovy fillets
8 ounces (225 grams) cream cheese, softened
2 tablespoons (30 milliliters) chopped parsley
1 teaspoon prepared mustard
2 tablespoons (30 milliliters) chopped capers
extra capers for garnishing

Cut the bread rounds with a 1½-inch (4-centimeter) cutter. Butter them.

Drain, dry, and finely chop the anchovies. Add the softened cream cheese, parsley, mustard and chopped capers; mix thoroughly. Spread on the prepared rounds. Top with a whole caper or two. Freeze on a cooky sheet or whatever fits into your freezer space. When frozen, put the canapés in freezer bags, label, and return to the freezer. *Makes 36 to 40 canapés. Storage time: 1 month.*

To use: Remove from freezer and put the canapés on a serving platter. Cover them with very damp paper towels. Thaw at room temperature for 1½ to 2 hours. Remove paper towels, decorate the platter, and serve.

CURRIED ANCHOVY CANAPÉS

1 loaf of white bread
4 ounces (115 grams) blue cheese
8 ounces (225 grams) cream cheese
1 ounce (30 grams) flat anchovy fillets
½ teaspoon curry powder
1 teaspoon ketchup

Cut the bread into rounds 1¾ inches (4½ centimeters) in diameter. Put them on a cooky sheet and into a 350° F. (180° C.) oven. Bake them for 5 to 6 minutes. They should be a little dry to the touch but should not take on any color as they will be baked again later on. Remove them, cover them with a dry towel, and allow them to cool.

Mash both cheeses together. Drain and finely chop the anchovies. Add them and all other ingredients to the cheeses. Mix well. Spread thinly on the toast rounds. Freeze the canapés on a cooky sheet or whatever fits into your freezer space. When frozen, put the canapés in freezer bags, label, and return to the freezer. *Makes about 50 canapés. Storage time: 1 month.*

To use: Bake the frozen canapés in a 350° F. (180° C.) oven for 8 to 10 minutes.

This mixture is great in turnovers.

BITE-SIZE FISH BALLS

8 ounces (225 grams) salt codfish
20 ounces (560 grams) raw potatoes, peeled and sliced (about 4
     medium-size potatoes)
1 onion, sliced
1 egg, beaten
1 tablespoon grated onion
1 teaspoon Worcestershire sauce
1 tablespoon butter
vegetable shortening for deep-frying
Cocktail Sauce, Rémoulade Sauce, or Mustard-Caper Sauce
     (see Index)

Cut the salt codfish into very small pieces with kitchen shears, or use a food processor. Put the fish in a saucepan and cover with cold water. Bring to a boil and drain off the water. When fish is cool enough to handle, pick it apart. Slice the potatoes, measure them, and put them and the sliced onion in the saucepan with the fish. Cover with cold water and bring to a boil. Boil until the potatoes are just cooked, not mushy. Drain thoroughly. Mash the fish, onion and potatoes together. Add the egg, grated onion, Worcestershire sauce and butter. Mix and mash until no sizeable lumps remain. Shape into small balls the size of a grape. Fry in deep fat heated to 385° F. (196° C.) for 30 to 40 seconds. They should be a nice golden color. Remove the fish balls and drain on brown paper. Cool. Put in freezer bags, label, and freeze. *Makes 50 to 60 fish balls. Storage time: 2 weeks.*

To use: Take as many fish balls out of the freezer as you want to use. Heat them on a cooky sheet in a 350° F. (180° C.) oven until heated through, 6 to 8 minutes. Serve hot with cocktail picks and one of the recommended sauces.

HERRING WITH PICKLED BEETS

1 large loaf of rye bread with caraway seeds
1½ ounces (45 grams) soft butter for bread rounds (⅛ tea-
    spoon per round)
8 ounces (225 grams) canned herring
4 ounces (115 grams) pimientos
6 tablespoons (¾ deciliter) finely minced pickled beets, drained
8 ounces (225 grams) cream cheese, softened
1 teaspoon dried dillweed

Cut out rounds with a 1½-inch (4-centimeter) cutter. Butter
them.

Drain the herring, pimientos and beets. Dry them all with paper
towels. Chop the herring and mince the pimientos and beets. Mix
them together with all the other ingredients. Blend thoroughly.
Heap on the prepared rounds. Freeze the canapés on a cooky sheet
or whatever fits best in your freezer space. When frozen, put the
canapés in freezer bags, label, and return to the freezer. *Makes about
60 canapés. Storage time: 3 weeks.*

To use: Put the frozen canapés on a serving platter and cover
with very damp paper towels. Thaw at room temperature for 1½ to
2 hours. Remove paper towels and serve.

To serve hot: Make toast rounds: Cut out the bread rounds with
a 1¾-inch (4½-centimeter) cutter. Put them into a preheated 350° F.
(180° C.) oven for 5 to 6 minutes. They should feel dry to the touch
but should not take on any color as they will be baked later on.

Mix the spread ingredients and mound on the rye toast rounds.
Freeze as directed.

To use: Bake in a preheated 350° F. (180° C.) oven until heated
through and bubbly, 10 to 15 minutes.

SMOKED SALMON CANAPÉS

1 loaf of white bread
1 to 1½ ounces (30 to 45 grams) soft butter for the rounds (⅛
    teaspoon per round)
3 ounces (90 grams) cream cheese
2 tablespoons (30 milliliters) dairy sour cream
2 ounces (60 grams) flat anchovy fillets, drained
2 ounces (60 grams) fresh smoked or canned smoked salmon,
    drained
ground pepper
capers, optional

Cut bread in rectangles 1¾ inches × 1 inch (4½ × 2½ centimeters) and butter them.

Mash the cheese and add the sour cream. With a sharp knife cut the anchovy fillets and the salmon into thin strips the same length as the bread rectangles. Place one of each, side by side, on the prepared bread. Press gently. Sprinkle with ground pepper to taste. With a pastry bag or tube, pipe a decorative line of softened cream cheese down the dividing line of the strips. Press 3 or 4 capers into the cheese. Freeze on a cooky sheet or whatever fits your freezer space. When frozen, put the canapés in freezer bags, label, and return to the freezer. *Makes 24 to 30 canapés. Storage time: 3 weeks.*

To use: Take from the freezer and carefully remove canapés from the bags. Place on a serving platter and cover them with very damp paper towels. Thaw at room temperature for 1½ to 2 hours. Remove paper towels and serve.

SALMON PINWHEELS

6½ ounces (195 grams) red (Sockeye) salmon, canned, or 6
    ounces (180 grams) poached fresh salmon
4 ounces (115 grams) Cheddar cheese
grated rind of 1 lemon
1 teaspoon lemon juice
½ teaspoon dried dillweed
ground pepper (I like quite a bit of pepper)
double recipe of Flaky Pastry (see Index)

Drain the salmon (if canned) and remove skin and bones. Mash the salmon. Add the rest of the ingredients except the pastry. Mix to a smooth paste.

Roll out the pastry to a rectangle ⅛ inch (½ centimeter) thick and approximately 20 × 9 inches (50 × 23 centimeters). Spread with the filling, keeping it ½ inch (1½ centimeters) in from both long sides. Spread it, however, right to the edge of the short sides. Cut into 2 pieces to make for easier handling. Roll up one piece from the originally long side to the other long side. Repeat with the other half. Wrap rolls in wax paper and chill thoroughly for 2 hours.

Unwrap rolls. With a very sharp knife, cut rolls into ½-inch (1½-centimeter) slices. Place the pinwheels on a cooky sheet or whatever fits into your storage place and freeze. When frozen, put the pinwheels in freezer bags, label, and return to the freezer. *Makes 35 to 40 pinwheels. Storage time: 3 weeks.*

To use: Bake the frozen pinwheels on a buttered cooky sheet with a raised edge. Set this sheet inside another one to keep the pinwheels from scorching on the bottom. Put them in a preheated 400° F. (205° C.) oven for 10 to 12 minutes, or until puffy and golden. Watch them carefully. In making these pinwheels, your nose will tell you when they are done, as they smell heavenly.

HOT SARDINE CANAPÉS

1 loaf of white bread
3¾ ounces (106 grams) canned boneless sardines
3 ounces (90 grams) cream cheese, softened
2 tablespoons (30 milliliters) dairy sour cream
6 stuffed green olives
1 teaspoon prepared mustard
1 tablespoon lemon juice
1 teaspoon grated lemon rind
pepper

Cut the bread rounds with a 1¾-inch (4½-centimeter) cutter, or make them any shape you wish with this approximate dimension. Put them on a cooky sheet and into a 350° F. (180° C.) oven for 5 or

6 minutes. They should get a little dry to the touch but should not take on any color as they will be baked later on. Remove them, cover them with a dry towel, and allow them to cool.

Drain and mash the sardines. Add the softened cream cheese and the sour cream. Mince the stuffed olives and add them, mustard, lemon juice and rind to the sardine mixture. Add pepper to taste and mix thoroughly. Heap on the toast rounds and freeze on a cooky sheet or whatever fits into your freezing space. When frozen, remove canapés from the freezer, put them in freezer bags, label, and return to the freezer. *Makes about 36 canapés. Storage time: 2 weeks.*

To use: Place the frozen sardine canapés in a 350° F. (180° C.) oven for 10 to 15 minutes, until hot and bubbly.

SOUFFLÉED SARDINE CANAPÉS

1 loaf of white bread
3¾ ounces (106 grams) canned brisling sardines
1 teaspoon prepared mustard
1 tablespoon mayonnaise
2 teaspoons minced parsley
½ teaspoon dried dillweed
2 egg whites

Cut the bread rounds with a 1¾-inch (4½-centimeter) cutter or make them any shape you wish. Put them on a cooky sheet and into a 350° F. (180° C.) oven for 5 to 6 minutes. They should be a little dry to the touch but should not take on any color as they will be baked later on.

Mash the sardines and add the mustard, mayonnaise, parsley and dill. Beat the egg whites until stiff. Fold egg whites gently into the sardine mixture. Heap the mixture on the toast rounds and freeze on a cooky sheet or whatever fits your freezer space. When frozen, put the canapés in freezer bags, label, and return to the freezer. *Makes about 20 canapés. Storage time: 3 weeks.*

To use: Remove frozen canapés from the freezer bags and place them on a cooky sheet. Bake in a 400° F. (205° C.) oven for about 10 minutes, or until puffed and golden. Or broil under medium heat for about 5 minutes, or until canapés are heated through, puffed and golden.

MUSTARD SARDINE CANAPÉS

1 loaf of white bread
1 ounce (30 grams) unsalted butter for rounds (⅛ teaspoon per
    round)
3¾ ounces (106 grams) canned small sardines
4 ounces (115 grams) unsalted butter, softened
2 tablespoons (30 milliliters) prepared mustard
1 teaspoon lemon juice
1 teaspoon ketchup
finely minced parsley, for garnish

Cut the white bread into rectangles a little longer than the sardines. Butter them.

Using the 4 ounces softened butter, mix it with the mustard, lemon juice and ketchup. Place a sardine on each rectangle and press it down gently to secure it. With a pastry bag or tube, pipe a border of the mustard butter around the sardine. With a demitasse spoon, sprinkle a bit of the minced parsley on the sardine, being careful not to get it on the mustard butter. There are between 25 and 35 sardines in a can so you can make that many canapés. Freeze the canapés on a cooky sheet or whatever fits your freezer space. When frozen, put the canapés in freezer bags, label, and return to the freezer. *Storage time: 2 weeks.*

To use: Put the frozen hors-d'oeuvre on a serving platter and cover with very damp paper towels. Thaw at room temperature for 1½ to 2 hours. Remove paper towels and serve.

CAVIAR CANAPÉS

1 loaf of white bread
1½ ounces (45 grams) soft butter for the rounds (⅛ teaspoon
    per round)
8 ounces (225 grams) cream cheese
4 ounces (115 grams) butter, softened
½ teaspoon dry mustard
½ teaspoon Worcestershire sauce

¼ teaspoon garlic powder
2 tablespoons (30 milliliters) minced parsley
3¾ ounces (106 grams) Danish lumpfish caviar, or real caviar
4 ounces (115 grams) pimientos

Cut out bread rounds with a 1½-inch (4-centimeter) cutter. Butter them. Even though there is a lot of butter in this recipe, the Worcestershire sauce and other ingredients can make the bread soggy, so you really do need the extra butter for the base.

Mix all ingredients together except the caviar and pimientos. Gently fold in the caviar. Spread on the prepared rounds. Top with a thin strip of pimiento. Freeze on a cooky sheet or whatever fits your freezer space. When frozen, put the canapés in freezer bags, label, and return to the freezer. *Makes about 50 canapés. Storage time: 2 weeks.*

To use: Take from the freezer, remove from bags, and place the frozen hors-d'oeuvre on a serving platter. Cover with very damp paper towels. Thaw at room temperature for 1½ to 2 hours. Remove paper towels and serve.

BLUE-CHEESE CAVIAR CANAPÉS

1 loaf of white bread
1 ounce (30 grams) soft butter for the rounds (⅛ teaspoon per round)
2 ounces (60 grams) blue cheese
4 ounces (115 grams) cream cheese
1 ounce (30 grams) softened butter
1 tablespoon dairy sour cream
½ teaspoon lemon juice
3¾ ounces (106 grams) Danish lumpfish caviar, or real caviar

Cut out bread rounds with a 1½-inch (4-centimeter) cutter or any shape you wish. Butter them.

Mash the cheeses and 1 ounce butter together, and add sour cream and lemon juice. Mix well. Heap the spread on the prepared rounds. Make an indentation in each one with a small spoon and place a little caviar in it. Press down gently with the spoon. Freeze on a cooky sheet or whatever fits your freezer space. When frozen, put the canapés in freezer bags, label, and return to the freezer. *Makes 25 to 30 canapés. Storage time: 2 weeks.*

To use: Take from the freezer and carefully remove canapés from the bags. Place on a serving platter and cover with very damp paper towels. Thaw at room temperature for 1½ to 2 hours. Remove paper towels and serve.

CAVIAR BOLOGNA CANAPÉS

1 loaf of whole-wheat bread
1½ ounces (45 grams) soft butter for the rounds (⅛ teaspoon
    per round)
12 ounces (340 grams) bologna
garlic powder
8 ounces (225 grams) cream cheese
3¾ ounces (106 grams) Danish lumpfish caviar

Cut out the bread rounds with a 1½-inch (4-centimeter) cutter. Butter them.

Cut bologna into the same size rounds as the bread, using the same cutter. Press the bologna slices firmly onto the buttered rounds. Sprinkle garlic powder to taste on the softened cream cheese. Mix well. With a pastry bag or tube, pipe the cream cheese a little in from the edge of the bologna all the way around. Fill the centers with a small amount of the caviar and press down gently with the back of a spoon. This may sound like a very strange combination of ingredients, but it really is delicious and one of my favorites.

Freeze on a cooky sheet or whatever fits your freezer space. When frozen, put the canapés in freezer bags, label, and return to the freezer. *Makes 30 to 35 canapés. Storage time: 2 weeks.*

To use: Take from the freezer and remove canapés from the bags, again being very careful of the caviar. Place frozen canapés on a serving platter and cover with very damp paper towels. Thaw at room temperature for 1½ to 2 hours. Remove paper towels and serve.

CAVIAR ANCHOVY CANAPÉS

1 loaf of white bread
1 ounce (30 grams) butter for bread rounds (⅛ teaspoon per
    round)

1 tablespoon dairy sour cream
3 ounces (90 grams) cream cheese
3¾ ounces (106 grams) Danish lumpfish caviar, or real caviar
2 ounces (60 grams) flat anchovy fillets

Cut the bread into rectangles 1 × 2 inches (2½ × 5 centimeters). Butter them.

Mix the sour cream with the cream cheese. Mound the cheese mixture on half of each rectangle and put caviar on the other half. Place a trimmed piece of anchovy across the middle where the halves meet. Freeze on a cooky sheet or whatever fits into your freezer space. When frozen, put the canapés in freezer bags, handling them carefully so as not to dislodge the caviar; label, and return to the freezer. *Makes 24 to 30 canapés. Storage time: 2 weeks.* These are very pretty canapés.

To use: Remove canapés from the freezer bags and, again being careful in handling them, arrange on a serving platter. Cover the canapés with very damp paper towels. Thaw at room temperature for 1½ to 2 hours. Remove towels and serve.

RED CAVIAR CELERY CANAPÉS

1 loaf of white bread
1½ ounces (45 grams) butter for the rounds (⅛ teaspoon per round)
8 ounces (225 grams) cream cheese (very soft)
2 tablespoons (30 milliliters) dairy sour cream
2 teaspoons grated onion
3 tablespoons (45 milliliters) grated celery
1 tablespoon minced parsley
½ teaspoon lemon juice
ground pepper
7½ ounces (217 grams) red caviar

Cut out the bread rounds with a 1½-inch (4-centimeter) cutter or in any desired shape. Butter them.

Mash the cream cheese. Add the sour cream, grated onion, grated celery, minced parsley, lemon juice and black pepper to taste. Gently fold in half of the red caviar. Chill for 1 hour.

Heap on the prepared rounds. Make an indentation with the back of a spoon and put a little caviar from the reserved half on each one. Freeze on a cooky sheet or whatever fits into your freezer space.

When frozen, put the canapés in freezer bags, label, and return to the freezer. *Makes about 50 canapés. Storage time: 1 to 2 weeks.*

To use: Place the frozen canapés on a serving platter and cover with very damp paper towels. Thaw at room temperature for 1½ to 2 hours. Remove paper towels and serve.

CLAMS IN PATTY SHELLS

8 ounces (225 grams) minced clams, canned or fresh-cooked
4 ounces (115 grams) Cheddar cheese, grated
1 teaspoon grated lemon rind
1 teaspoon Worcestershire sauce
1 tablespoon minced chives
salt
lemon marinade or ground pepper
50 patty shells (see Patty Shells recipe)

Drain the clams and mash the Cheddar cheese. Mix them and all other ingredients except patty shells together thoroughly. Use seasonings to taste.

Make the patty shells. Put a small amount of the clam mixture in the center of each patty shell. Put patties on a cooky sheet or whatever fits your freezer space, and freeze them. When frozen, put the patties in freezer bags, label, and return them to the freezer. *Makes 50 patties. Storage time: 2 weeks.*

To use: Place frozen patties on a buttered cooky sheet set inside another cooky sheet, and bake them in a preheated 400° F. (205° C.) oven for 10 to 15 minutes. The sides of the patty shell will rise up around the filling and will be golden and puffy.

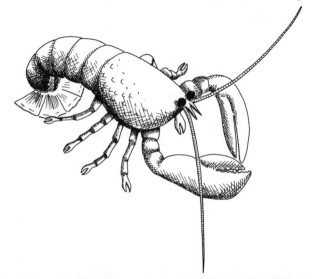

DOWN EAST CLAM SPREAD AND CANAPÉS

8 ounces (225 grams) minced clams, canned or fresh
2 ounces (60 grams) butter
8 ounces (225 grams) cream cheese
2 teaspoons anchovy paste
1 teaspoon lemon juice
1 tablespoon minced chives
1 teaspoon Worcestershire sauce
parsley or other green for garnish

As spread: Drain the clams. Mince clams even more. Mash the butter and cheese together and add all other ingredients except garnish. Mix thoroughly and put in a freezer container, label, and freeze. *Serves 10 people. Storage time: 2 weeks.*

To use: Remove from freezer to refrigerator 24 hours before needed. Mash with a fork and shape on a serving platter into a log or whatever you wish. Garnish with the parsley and serve with crackers.

As canapés:

1 loaf of oatmeal or wheat bread
1½ ounces (45 grams) butter for the rounds (⅛ teaspoon per round)

Cut the bread rounds with a 1½-inch (4-centimeter) cutter. Butter them.

Mix the ingredients as before, only reserve the greens for garnish. Heap the spread on the bread rounds and sprinkle chives on top. You may need as much as 4 tablespoons snipped chives to cover them all. Press down gently to secure chives. Freeze on a cooky sheet. When frozen, carefully put canapés in freezer bags, label, and return to the freezer. *Makes about 50 canapés. Storage time: 2 weeks.*

To use: Take from the freezer and remove canapés carefully from the bags. Place frozen canapés on a serving platter and cover with very damp paper towels. Thaw at room temperature for 1½ to 2 hours. Remove the paper towels and serve.

SMOKED BABY CLAM CANAPÉS, HOT

1 loaf of white bread
3½ ounces (100 grams) canned smoked baby clams
4 ounces (115 grams) Cheddar cheese, grated
1 tablespoon minced chives
¼ teaspoon lemon juice
ground pepper

Cut bread rounds with a 1¾-inch (4½-centimeter) cutter. Put them on a cooky sheet and into a 350° F. (180° C.) oven for 5 to 6 minutes. They should feel dry to the touch but should not take on any color as they will be baked again later on. Remove rounds from the oven and cover with a dry towel. Allow the rounds to cool.

Finely chop the clams. Mix with all the other ingredients. Use pepper to taste. Mix until well blended. Spread on the toast rounds and freeze on a cooky sheet or whatever fits best in your freezer space. When frozen, put the canapés in freezer bags, label, and return to the freezer. *Makes about 36 canapés. Storage time: 2 weeks.*

To use: Bake the frozen canapés on a cooky sheet in a 400° F. (205° C.) oven for 8 to 10 minutes, or until puffy and starting to brown.

CLAM ANCHOVY CANAPÉS

1 loaf of white bread
1½ ounces (45 grams) soft butter for the rounds (⅛ teaspoon per round)
8 ounces (225 grams) minced clams, canned or fresh-cooked
1 ounce (30 grams) flat anchovy fillets
¼ teaspoon garlic powder
½ teaspoon curry powder
8 ounces (225 grams) cream cheese
parsley

Cut out the bread rounds with a 1½-inch (4-centimeter) cutter or any shape you wish. Butter them.

Finely chop the minced clams and anchovy fillets. Mix

thoroughly with all other ingredients except parsley. Heap on the prepared rounds. Decorate each one with a small piece of parsley. Freeze on a cooky sheet or whatever fits your freezer space. When frozen, put the canapés in freezer bags, label, and return to the freezer. Handle with care. *Makes about 50 canapés. Storage time: 2 weeks.*

To use: Take from the freezer and remove canapés carefully from the bags. Place them on a serving platter and cover with very damp paper towels. Thaw at room temperature for 1½ to 2 hours. Remove paper towels and serve.

SMOKED MUSSELS WITH CREAM CHEESE
(Spread or Dip)

1 loaf of white bread
1½ ounces (45 grams) butter for rounds (⅛ teaspoon per round)
4 ounces (115 grams) canned smoked mussels
4 ounces (115 grams) cream cheese
½ teaspoon prepared mustard
1 tablespoon anchovy paste
capers, for garnish

This spread can be frozen in a 1-quart (1-liter) freezer container to be spread on bread rounds another day.

Cut bread rounds with a 1½-inch (4-centimeter) cutter, and butter them.

Drain and finely chop the mussels. Mash the cheese with a fork and add the mussels to it. Add mustard and anchovy paste. Mix well and spread on the prepared rounds. Put 1 or 2 capers on each one. Freeze the canapés on a cooky sheet or whatever fits your freezer space. When frozen, put the canapés in freezer bags, label, and return to the freezer. *Makes about 36 canapés. Storage time: 2 weeks.*

To use: Put the frozen canapés on a serving platter and cover with very damp paper towels. Thaw at room temperature for 1½ to 2 hours. Remove paper towels and serve.

To serve as a dip: Mix as directed above and put in a 2-cup (½-liter) container, label, and freeze.

To use: Remove from freezer 24 hours before needed. Thaw in refrigerator. Beat with a fork and add only as much sour cream as needed to give the right consistency for a dip. Put in a pretty bowl and surround with interesting crackers or chips. *Serves 8 to 10 people.*

OYSTER DIP

8 ounces (225 grams) cream cheese
8 ounces (225 grams) oysters, canned or fresh
1 tablespoon dairy sour cream
4 teaspoons Worcestershire sauce
2 tablespoons (30 milliliters) snipped chives
½ teaspoon seasoned salt
1 teaspoon paprika
1 tablespoon lemon juice
2 tablespoons (30 milliliters) chopped capers

Mash the cheese. Mince the oysters and save the juice from the can. Add all the other ingredients. Dips thin out in the freezing process so add only as much of the oyster juice as needed to make it a very thick dip. If dip is too thin, it will not stay on a cracker or potato chip but will run off and be messy. Put the dip in a 1-quart (1-liter) freezer container, label, and freeze. *Serves about 10 people. Storage time: 2 weeks.*

To use: Thaw in the refrigerator for 24 hours. Whisk the dip with a fork or wire whisk. Serve in a bowl surrounded with slivers of fresh vegetables or chips.

OYSTER CANAPÉS I

1 loaf of Anadama or oatmeal bread
2 ounces (60 grams) soft butter for bread rounds (⅛ teaspoon
   per round)
5 ounces (140 grams) oysters, canned or fresh
8 ounces (225 grams) cream cheese
¼ teaspoon garlic powder
few drops of Worcestershire sauce
1 teaspoon anchovy paste
lemon peel slivers from 1 lemon

This spread can be frozen in a 1-quart (1-liter) freezer container to be spread on the rounds another day.

Cut out the bread rounds with a 1½-inch (4-centimeter) cutter, or any shape you choose. Butter them.

Drain the oysters, if canned, and finely chop them. Add all other ingredients except lemon peel and mix thoroughly. Heap on the prepared rounds. Top with little slivers of lemon peel. Freeze on a cooky sheet or whatever fits into your freezer space. When frozen, put the canapés in freezer bags, label, and return to the freezer. *Makes about 60 canapés. Storage time: 2 weeks.*

To use: Remove canapés from the freezer and place on a serving platter. Cover them with very damp paper towels. Thaw at room temperature for 1½ to 2 hours. Remove paper towels and serve.

To freeze in a container: Put the mixture, without the lemon peel, in a 1-quart (1-liter) freezer container, label, and freeze.

To use: Remove from the freezer 24 hours before you want to serve the oyster spread. Thaw in the refrigerator. Place on a serving platter and mold it into a long log or some other rectangular shape. Surround with crackers or buttered bread rounds and decorate with the slivers of lemon peel. *Serves about 10 people.*

OYSTER CANAPÉS II

1 loaf of white bread
2 ounces (60 grams) soft butter for bread rounds (⅛ teaspoon
    per round)
5 ounces (140 grams) oysters, canned or fresh
8 ounces (225 grams) cream cheese
1 tablespoon chili sauce
1 teaspoon prepared horseradish, drained
1 teaspoon lemon juice
¼ teaspoon dried dillweed
salt and ground pepper
lemon peel slivers from 1 lemon, for garnish

This spread can be frozen in a 1-quart (1-liter) freezer container to be spread on rounds another day.

Cut out the bread rounds with a 1½-inch (4-centimeter) cutter, or make them any shape you wish. Butter them.

Drain and finely chop the oysters. Add all other ingredients except lemon peel. Spread on the prepared bread rounds and top with a tiny sliver of lemon peel measuring ½ x ¹/₁₆ inch (1½ x ¼ centimeter). Freeze on a cooky sheet or whatever fits into your freezer space. When frozen, put the canapés in freezer bags, label, and return to the freezer. *Makes 50 to 60 canapés. Storage time: 2 weeks.*

To use: Take frozen hors-d'oeuvre from the freezer and place on a serving platter. Cover with very damp paper towels. Thaw at room temperature for 1½ to 2 hours. Remove the paper towels and serve.

To freeze in a container: Mix the spread as in the recipe but blend 2 to 3 teaspoons of finely minced lemon slivers into the spread. Label the freezer container and freeze.

To use: Remove the container from the freezer 24 hours before needed. Thaw in the refrigerator. Place the mixture on a serving platter and shape or mold it into a ball, log, or flattened oval. Decorate it with a few slivers of lemon peel. *Serves 10 to 12 people.*

OYSTER ANCHOVY CANAPÉS

1 loaf of white bread
1½ to 2 ounces (45 to 60 grams) soft butter for the rounds (⅛
    teaspoon per round)
8 ounces (225 grams) canned oysters, drained
1 ounce flat anchovy fillets, drained
8 ounces (225 grams) cream cheese
1 tablespoon chopped parsley
ground pepper
parsley for garnish

This spread can be frozen in a 1-quart (1-liter) freezer container to be spread on the rounds another day.

Cut out the bread rounds with a 1½-inch (4-centimeter) cutter. Butter them.

Chop oysters and anchovies. Add to the softened cream cheese. Add parsley and pepper to taste; mix well. Heap on the prepared bread rounds. Top each with a sprig of parsley. Freeze on a cooky sheet or whatever fits into your freezer space. When frozen, put the canapés in freezer bags, label, and return to the freezer. *Makes about 60 canapés. Storage time: 2 weeks.*

To use: Remove from the freezer and place canapés on a serving platter. Cover with very damp paper towels. Thaw at room temperature for 1½ to 2 hours. Remove paper towels and serve.

If the mixture was frozen in a freezer container, thaw in the container in the refrigerator for 24 hours. Put on a serving platter and shape into a roll or some other shape. Decorate with parsley and serve.

HOT OYSTER BACON CANAPÉS

1 loaf of white bread
8 ounces (225 grams) oysters, canned or fresh
4 ounces (115 grams) Cheddar cheese, grated
2 tablespoons (30 milliliters) snipped chives
3 strips of raw bacon, chopped
½ teaspoon grated lemon rind
ground pepper

Cut the bread slices with a 1¾-inch (4½-centimeter) cutter or any shape you desire. Put them on a cooky sheet and into a preheated oven set at 350° F. (180° C.). Leave the rounds for 5 to 6 minutes. They should be dry to the touch but should not take on any color as they will be baked again later on. Remove the rounds from the oven, cover with a dry towel, and allow them to cool.

Drain and mince the oysters and mix them with all other ingredients. Pile lightly on the toast rounds, put them on a cooky sheet, and freeze. When frozen, put the canapés in freezer bags, label, and return to the freezer. *Do not keep them in the freezer longer than 2 to 3 weeks. Makes about 55 canapés.*

To use: Bake the frozen canapés in a preheated oven set at 350° F. (180° C.) for 10 to 15 minutes, or broil them until they are heated through and brown and bubbly.

VARIATION:

8 ounces (225 grams) oysters, canned or fresh
4 ounces (115 grams) Cheddar cheese, grated
2 tablespoons chili sauce
3 strips of raw bacon, chopped
½ teaspoon curry powder
½ teaspoon ground mace

Proceed as directed in the basic recipe. *Also makes about 55 canapés. Storage time: 2 weeks.*

COLD CRAB-MEAT CANAPÉS

1 loaf of white bread
1½ ounces (45 grams) soft butter for rounds (⅛ teaspoon per
    round)
8 ounces (225 grams) fresh or canned crab meat
8 ounces (225 grams) cream cheese
1 tablespoon lemon juice
grated rind of ½ lemon
1 tablespoon grated onion
2 tablespoons (30 milliliters) chili sauce
2 tablespoons (30 milliliters) Worcestershire sauce
¼ teaspoon dried dillweed
garlic powder
salt and pepper
parsley

This spread can be frozen in a 1-quart (1-liter) freezer container
to be put on rounds another day.

Cut out the bread rounds with a 1½-inch (4-centimeter) cutter.
Butter them.

Remove any cartilage and bone from the crab meat and chop
the meat finely. Mash the cheese and add it and all other ingredients
to the crab meat; mix well. Use seasonings to taste. Spread on the
prepared rounds. Top with parsley. Freeze on a cooky sheet or
whatever fits your freezer space. When frozen, put the canapés in
freezer bags, label, and return to the freezer. *Makes about 50 canapés.
Storage time: 2 weeks.*

To use: Take from the freezer and remove canapés carefully
from the bags. Place them on a serving platter and cover with very
damp paper towels. Thaw at room temperature for 1½ to 2 hours.
Remove paper towels and serve.

If the crab-meat spread was frozen in a container, take it from
the freezer 24 hours before you want to use it. Fluff it up with a fork
and spread on bread rounds; or mound it on a serving platter and
surround with crackers or Melba toast.

HOT CRAB-MEAT CANAPÉS

    1 loaf of white bread
    8 ounces (225 grams) fresh or canned crab meat
    4 ounces (115 grams) cream cheese
    1 ounce (30 grams) Cheddar cheese, grated
    1 tablespoon snipped chives
    1 teaspoon Worcestershire sauce

Cut out the bread rounds with a 1¾-inch (4½-centimeter) cutter or any shape you wish. Put them on a cooky sheet and into a preheated 350° F. (180° C.) oven. Leave them for 5 to 6 minutes. They should be a little dry to the touch but should not take on any color as they will be baked later on. Remove the rounds, cover them with a dry towel, and allow to cool.

Remove any cartilage and bone from the crab meat. Mash both cheeses with a fork. Mix them thoroughly with all other ingredients. Heap on the toast rounds. Freeze on a cooky sheet or whatever fits into your freezer space. When frozen, put the canapés in freezer bags, label, and return to the freezer. *Makes about 50 canapés. Storage time: 2 weeks.*

To use: Bake the frozen hors-d'oeuvre in a 400° F. (205° C.) oven for 8 to 10 minutes, or until they are golden and bubbly.

SPICY CRAB-MEAT PATTIES

    4 ounces (115 grams) crab meat, fresh or canned
    8 ounces (225 grams) cream cheese
    ½ small garlic clove, put through a press
    1 teaspoon Worcestershire sauce
    1 teaspoon minced onion
    1 teaspoon prepared horseradish, drained
    1 teaspoon mayonnaise
    1 teaspoon lemon juice
    salt and ground pepper
    50 patty shells (see Patty Shells recipe)

Remove any cartilage and bone from the crab meat. Mash the cream cheese with a fork and add the crab meat and all other ingredients to it, except patty shells. Mix well.

Prepare the patty shells according to the directions in that recipe. Place the prepared pastry rounds on a cooky sheet and put a small mound of the crab-meat mixture in the center. Try not to get the filling on the rim of the shell. Freeze on a cooky sheet or whatever fits into your freezer space. When frozen, put the pastries in a freezer bag, label, and return to the freezer until needed. *Makes about 50 patties. Storage time: 3 weeks.*

To use: Bake the patties on a buttered cooky sheet with a raised edge in a 400° F. (205° C.) oven for 10 to 15 minutes. The sides of the patty shells should rise high around the filling and be puffed and golden.

HOT CRAB-MEAT TURNOVERS

Flaky Pastry (see Index)
8 ounces (225 grams) fresh or canned crab meat
1 ounce (30 grams) butter
1 medium-size onion, minced
¼ cup (½ deciliter) minced green pepper
3 tablespoons unbleached flour
1 cup (¼ liter) milk
3 flat anchovy fillets, minced
1½ ounces (45 milliliters) sherry
2 ounces (60 grams) Cheddar cheese, grated
pinch of dried thyme
salt and ground pepper
1 egg mixed with 2 teaspoons water

Prepare the pastry and roll it out ⅛ inch (½ centimeter) thick. Cut into 2½-inch (6½-centimeter) rounds.

Drain crab meat and remove cartilage. Melt the butter and sauté the onion and green pepper in it over medium-low heat, until the onion is golden and the green pepper almost tender. Add flour and cook and stir for 2 minutes. Gradually add the milk. Add all other ingredients except egg, and cook, stirring, until very thick. Cool.

Place a little of the mixture on a pastry round. Brush a little of the egg mixture around the edges, fold one half over the other, and seal the edges. Press the edges together firmly. Freeze on a cooky sheet or whatever fits into your freezer space. When frozen, put the turnovers in freezer bags, label, and return to the freezer. *Makes about 40 turnovers. Storage time: 3 weeks.*

To use: With a sharp knife make a small slit in the top of each turnover. Bake on a cooky sheet, placed on another cooky sheet, in a 400° F. (205° C.) oven for 10 to 15 minutes, until golden and puffy.

LOBSTER MUSHROOM CANAPÉS
(Cold or Hot)

1 loaf of Anadama bread
2 ounces (60 grams) butter for the rounds (⅛ teaspoon per round)
6 small mushrooms
8 ounces (225 grams) cooked or canned lobster meat, finely chopped
8 ounces (225 grams) cream cheese
1 tablespoon mayonnaise
1 tablespoon chili sauce
1 teaspoon dried dillweed
½ teaspoon prepared mustard
1 teaspoon sour pickle
parsley, for garnish

This recipe can be frozen in a 1-quart (1-liter) freezer container to be spread on rounds another day.

Cut out bread rounds with a 1½-inch (4-centimeter) cutter, or make them some other shape with this approximate dimension. Butter them.

Wipe the mushrooms clean and mince them. Mix all ingredients together and heap on the prepared rounds. Decorate each canapé with a piece of parsley. If you wish, you may reserve a small piece of lobster before chopping it, and cut the reserved piece into smaller pieces to decorate the canapés. Freeze on a cooky sheet or whatever fits into your freezer space. When frozen, put canapés carefully in freezer bags, label, and return to the freezer. *Makes about 50 canapés. Storage time: 2 weeks.*

To use: Take from the freezer and carefully remove canapés from the freezer bags. Place them on a serving platter and cover with very damp paper towels. Thaw at room temperature for 1½ to 2 hours. Remove paper towels and serve.

To serve hot: Cut out bread rounds 1¾ inches (4½ centimeters) in diameter. Place them on a cooky sheet and into a 350° F. (180° C.) oven for 5 to 6 minutes. They should be a little dry to the touch but should not take on any color as they will be baked again later on. Remove the rounds and cover with a dry towel. Allow them to cool.

Heap the mixture on the toast rounds and freeze on a cooky sheet or whatever fits into your freezer space. When frozen, put the canapés in freezer bags, label, and return to the freezer.

To use: Bake in a 350° F. (180° C.) oven for 10 to 12 minutes, or until heated through and bubbly.

SHRIMP CANAPÉS

1 loaf of white bread
1 to 1½ ounces (30 to 45 grams) butter for the bread rounds
   (⅛ teaspoon per round)
2 pounds (900 grams) small Maine shrimps, or 1 pound (450
   grams) large shrimps
½ pound (225 grams) butter
1 ounce (30 milliliters) sherry

Cut out bread rounds with a 1½-inch (4-centimeter) cutter. Butter them.

Cook shrimps in a small amount of boiling water—2 minutes (after the boil) for Maine shrimps, or 10 to 15 minutes for the larger shrimps. Drain and cool. Shell them, devein the large shrimps, and reserve shrimps and shells. Put some hot water in a blender, pour out, and dry blender thoroughly. Melt the butter and pour it into the warm blender. Add the shells, a few at a time, until they are all puréed. Press the mixture through a sieve with a wooden spoon. Add the sherry.

Chop up the shrimps, keeping enough whole Maine shrimps to decorate the canapés. The larger ones will have to be cut into smaller pieces, but keep out enough for garnish. Add the chopped shrimps to the shrimp butter and mix well. Spread on the prepared rounds and put the reserved pieces of shrimp on top. Freeze on a cooky sheet or whatever fits your freezer space. When frozen, put the canapés in freezer bags, label, and return to the freezer. *Makes about 60 canapés. Storage time: 2 weeks.*

To use: Take canapés from the freezer and remove from the bags. Place the frozen hors-d'oeuvre on a serving platter and cover with very damp paper towels. Thaw at room temperature for 2 hours. Remove paper towels and serve.

SHRIMP MUSHROOM CANAPÉS

2 tablespoons minced onion
3 ounces (90 grams) butter
8 ounces (225 grams) mushrooms
2 tablespoons unbleached flour
¾ cup (1½ deciliters) milk
1 ounce (30 milliliters) sherry
pinch of grated nutmeg
½ teaspoon salt
¼ teaspoon lemon juice
6 large shrimps, cooked, shelled, deveined and finely minced
Flaky Pastry rounds (see Index), or 1 loaf of Anadama or white
    bread
1 to 1½ ounces (30 to 45 grams) soft butter, if bread is used in
    place of the pastry (⅛ teaspoon per round)
parsley

Sauté onion in 1½ ounces of the butter over medium high heat, stirring constantly, for 5 minutes. Onion should be golden brown. Reduce the heat and add the mushrooms which should be wiped clean and finely minced. Cook for 5 minutes, stirring once in awhile. Add flour and cook for a few more minutes. Slowly stir in the milk, sherry, nutmeg, salt and lemon juice. Cook until thick. Remove from heat and cool.

Put some hot water in a blender, pour it out, and dry the blender well. Melt another 1½ ounces of butter and pour it into the warm blender with the minced shrimps. Purée at high speed. This makes a smooth shrimp paste.

Make the pastry and roll it out ⅛ inch (½ centimeter) thick. Cut into 1¾-inch (4½-centimeter) rounds. Place the rounds on a cooky sheet and prick them all over with a fork. Bake the rounds in a 375° F. (190° C.) oven for 12 to 15 minutes, until golden. If you use bread rounds, cut them a little smaller—1½ inches (4 centimeters) in diameter. Butter the bread rounds.

With a pastry bag or tube, using a large enough opening to pass the tiny pieces of shrimp, pipe a border of the shrimp paste on the pastry rounds or buttered bread rounds. Fill the centers with the mushroom mixture. Decorate each one with a piece of parsley. Freeze on a cooky sheet or whatever fits your freezer space. When frozen, put the canapés in freezer bags, label, and return to the freezer. *Makes about 40 canapés. Storage time: 2 to 3 weeks.*

To use, if pastry: Take from the freezer and carefully remove the canapés from the bags. Place them on a serving platter and cover with paper towels. Thaw at room temperature for 1½ to 2 hours. Remove paper towels and serve.

To use, if bread rounds: Take canapés from the freezer and arrange on a serving platter. Cover with very damp paper towels. Thaw at room temperature for 1½ to 2 hours. Remove paper towels and serve.

SHRIMP BUTTER

8 ounces (225 grams) butter
2 cups (½ liter) firmly packed shrimp shells, left over from a
 shrimp recipe
salt and white pepper
1 ounce (30 milliliters) sherry

This recipe is not nearly as difficult to do as it may sound. The only troublesome part is putting the mixture through a strainer, but the results are so good that I am sure you will find it well worth the effort. Shrimp butter is superb served in a small crock and surrounded by crackers. It is also good in other canapé mixtures and as an addition to sauces.

Warm the blender by pouring very hot water into it. Pour it out and dry the blender. Melt the butter; when very hot, pour it into the blender. Add a few shrimp shells and blend at high speed; add a few shells at a time until all are used. Still on high speed, add salt and pepper to taste. Strain the butter into a bowl, using a wooden spoon to press the mixture through the strainer. Add the sherry. Taste for seasoning and add a little more sherry if needed. Chill, stirring once or twice as butter hardens. Put in a crock or other 8-ounce (225-gram) serving container. Freeze, using a piece of foil for a cover.

This butter may be used the way you would any pâté. I always make it when I have a molded shrimp pâté and use it, with a few whole shrimps, to decorate the pâté. It is a lovely pink color and goes easily through a pastry bag or tube.

To use: Remove butter from the freezer and put it in the refrigerator for 24 hours before you want to use it. When thawed, put the crock or other container of shrimp butter on a serving platter and surround it with interesting, rather plain crackers. *Serves 10 to 15 people.*

SHRIMP PÂTÉ I

1 pound (450 grams) shrimps, cooked and shelled
1 ounce (30 grams) flat anchovy fillets
1 ounce (30 grams) butter
3 ounces (90 grams) cream cheese
2 ounces (60 milliliters) dry white wine or vermouth
¼ teaspoon dried dillweed
½ teaspoon lemon juice
freshly ground pepper
parsley, minced

Put all ingredients except the parsley in a blender and blend at high speed until mixture is a smooth paste. Or put in a bowl and mash and pound it together until you achieve the same result. Use black pepper to taste. Spoon into a 1-quart (1-liter) freezer container, label, and freeze. *Serves 6 to 8 people. Storage time: 2 to 3 weeks.*

To use: Thaw in the refrigerator for 24 hours. Remove pâté from the freezer container and place it on a serving platter. Shape it into a long roll. Put a line of finely chopped parsley down the center and put a couple of large sprigs at both ends.

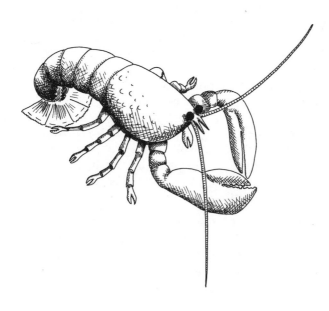

SHRIMP PÂTÉ II

3 loaves of party pumpernickel bread
1 loaf of white bread
3 ounces (90 grams) butter for the rounds (⅛ teaspoon per
    round)
3 pounds (1.35 kilograms) shrimps, cooked and shelled
4 ounces (115 grams) butter
¼ cup (½ deciliter) dairy sour cream
1 teaspoon wine vinegar
4 tablespoons (60 milliliters) anchovy paste
¾ cup (1½ deciliters) snipped chives
3 ounces (90 grams) cream cheese
1½ ounces (45 milliliters) sherry
salt and ground pepper
parsley

Cut the crusts off the party pumpernickel bread. This bread is about 3 inches (8 centimeters) in diameter; each slice makes 2 generous canapés. Cut the trimmed slices into halves and butter them. Cut the white bread with a 1½-inch (4-centimeter) cutter and butter these rounds. Cut 100 "rounds" altogether.

Reserve a few shrimps for decoration and put the rest of the shrimps through the finest blade of a meat grinder. Mix together all the other ingredients except the parsley. Use salt and pepper to taste. (The parsley you will not freeze but will have available the day of your party.) Add the mixture to the ground shrimps and mix thoroughly. Put in two 1-quart (1-liter) containers, label, and freeze. *Serves about 25 people. Storage time: 1 month.*

Put the buttered bread rounds on a cooky sheet, or whatever fits into your freezer space, and put it in the freezer. When frozen, put the bread rounds in freezer bags, label, and return to the freezer.

Put the reserved shrimps in a freezer bag and press the air out of it. Label and freeze.

To use: Place the container of shrimp pâté and the bag of reserved shrimps in the refrigerator for 24 hours. At 4 hours before your party take the bread rounds from the freezer. Fluff the shrimp pâté with a fork and mold it in any desired shape on a very large serving platter. Decorate it with the reserved shrimps. Place the bread rounds around the pâté. Cover the whole platter with very damp paper towels. Cover towels with plastic wrap and return the platter to the refrigerator.

NOTE: This may be prepared in the usual way: spread the bread rounds before freezing, decorate with the reserved shrimps, and freeze them. *Makes 100 canapés.*

CHICKEN

Why anyone would want to raise those clucking, pecking, antagonistic creatures, I'll never know. However, I'm very glad that some people do because eggs and chicken are popular items at our house, in the refrigerator and freezer.

In hors-d'oeuvre, the combination of chicken, mushrooms, aromatic herbs, sweet butter and spices is certainly a savory treat. To add curry, chutney and cream cheese to the same old bird is to put her in the category of food fit for kings and presidents.

Most people enjoy chicken in all its forms. Chicken liver pâté with brandied raisins is a special favorite of mine. If I had included all my ideas for chicken recipes, this book would resemble the New York telephone book, so I've just selected a few and hope that it will spur you on to create some new ones of your own.

HOT CHICKEN ALMOND CANAPÉS
(for a large cocktail party)

1 loaf of white bread
1 pound (450 grams) cooked chicken
2¾ ounces (78 grams) whole unblanched almonds
2 ounces (60 grams) butter
5 tablespoons (½ deciliter) heavy cream
½ teaspoon ground rosemary
1 tablespoon tomato paste
1 tablespoon minced shallot or onion
1 ounce (30 milliliters) sherry
¼ teaspoon dried tarragon
4½ ounces (130 grams) canned deviled ham
1 egg, beaten
salt and pepper

Cut out the bread rounds with a 1¾-inch (4½-centimeter) cutter or any shape you wish. Put them on a cooky sheet and into a pre-heated 350° F. (180° C.) oven. Leave them for 5 to 6 minutes. They should be a little dry to the touch, but they should not take on any color as they will be baked later on. Remove the rounds, cover with a dry towel, and allow them to cool.

Put chicken and almonds through the finest blade of a meat grinder, and add all other ingredients. Use salt and pepper to taste. Heap on the toast rounds, and freeze on a cooky sheet or whatever fits your freezer space. When frozen, put the canapés in freezer bags, label, and return to the freezer. *Makes about 100 canapés.*

To use: Preheat oven to 400° F. (205° C.). Bake the canapés on a cooky sheet for 8 to 10 minutes, or until they are brown and bubbly. NOTE: You should allow 5 or 6 assorted canapés per person at a cocktail party. This recipe would be one of several other kinds, so you might allow 2 or 3 of these per person. This recipe might be used for a party of 30 or more people. If you are having a party for fewer guests, then take however many canapés you think you will need from the freezer bags and return the rest to the freezer for another day.

COLD CHICKEN ALMOND CANAPÉS

1 loaf of Anadama bread or other slightly sweet bread
2½ ounces (75 grams) soft butter for rounds (⅛ teaspoon per
round)
2¾ ounces (78 grams) whole unblanched almonds
1 pound (450 grams) cooked chicken, ground
2 ounces (60 grams) butter
5 tablespoons (½ deciliter) cream
½ teaspoon ground rosemary
1 tablespoon tomato paste
1 ounce (30 milliliters) sherry
¼ teaspoon tarragon
salt and pepper

This recipe is a variation of Hot Chicken Almond Canapés.

Cut out the bread rounds with a 1½-inch (4-centimeter) cutter, or make them any shape you wish. Butter them.

Put almonds on a cooky sheet and toast them in a 400° F. (205° C.) oven. Watch them carefully so they do not burn. Whole unblanched almonds are brown to start with, so you have to go by the smell to know when to take them out. About 5 minutes should do it.

Mix together all the ingredients except the almonds. Use salt and pepper to taste. Heap on the prepared rounds. Put a toasted almond on each one. Freeze on a cooky sheet. When frozen, put canapés in freezer bags, label, and return them to the freezer. *Makes 60 to 70 canapés. Storage time: 2 weeks.*

To use: Take canapés from the freezer and carefully remove them from the bags. Arrange them on a serving platter and cover them with very damp paper towels. Thaw at room temperature for 1½ to 2 hours. Remove paper towels and serve.

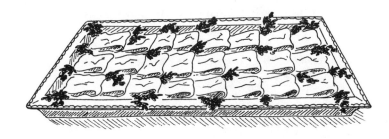

CHICKEN ARTICHOKE CANAPÉS

1 loaf of Anadama or oatmeal bread
1 ounce (30 grams) soft butter (⅛ teaspoon per round)
14 ounces (400 grams) canned artichoke hearts
8 ounces (225 grams) cooked chicken, finely ground
4 ounces (115 grams) butter
½ teaspoon dried tarragon
2 teaspoons tomato paste
1 teaspoon A.1. Sauce or Worcestershire sauce
salt and pepper
parsley

Cut out the bread rounds with a 1½-inch (4-centimeter) cutter. Butter them.

Slice the artichoke hearts crosswise into 3 or 4 pieces, depending on their size. Set aside. Mix all other ingredients together except parsley. Use salt and pepper to taste. Spread the mixture thickly on the prepared rounds. Place a slice of artichoke heart on the chicken mixture and press down gently to secure it. Decorate each canapé with a piece of parsley. Place them on a cooky sheet or whatever fits your freezer space and freeze. When frozen, put the canapés in freezer bags, label, and return to the freezer. *Makes about 24 canapés. Storage time: 1 month.*

To use: Take canapés from the freezer and carefully remove from the bags. Arrange them on a serving platter and cover them with very damp paper towels. Thaw at room temperature for 1½ to 2 hours. Remove paper towels and serve.

CHICKEN MUSHROOM CANAPÉS

1 loaf of Anadama bread
2¾ ounces (78 grams) slivered blanched almonds
8 ounces (225 grams) cooked chicken
4 or 5 medium-size mushrooms
2 ounces (60 grams) cream cheese
1 tablespoon mayonnaise
⅛ teaspoon dried tarragon
1 ounce (30 milliliters) sherry or Madeira
salt and pepper

Cut out bread rounds with a 1¾-inch (4½-centimeter) cutter. Put them on a cooky sheet and into a 350° F. (180° C.) oven. Leave them for 5 or 6 minutes. They should be a little dry to the touch but should not take on any color as they will be baked again later on. Remove the rounds, cover them with a dry towel, and allow to cool.

Increase oven temperature to 400° F. (205° C.) Toast the almonds on a cooky sheet until they are golden. Do not let them get too brown or they will be bitter. Remove from oven and cool.

Put the cooked chicken through the finest blade of a meat grinder. Chop half the almonds, reserving the rest. Chop the mushrooms, stems and all, after wiping them clean with a damp cloth. Put all the ingredients together and mix thoroughly. Use salt and pepper to taste. Heap on the toast rounds. Sprinkle reserved slivered almonds on top; press down to secure. Freeze on a cooky sheet. When frozen, put the canapés in freezer bags, label, and return to the freezer. *Makes about 35 canapés. Storage time: 1 month.*

To use: Bake frozen canapés in a 400° F. (205° C.) oven for 8 to 10 minutes, or until brown and bubbly.

VARIATION:
COLD CHICKEN MUSHROOM CANAPÉS

Assemble the ingredients in the basic recipe.

> 1 tablespoon butter
> small pinch of grated nutmeg
> garnish: parsley, slivered almonds, tiny pieces of fresh orange peel
> 1½ ounces (45 grams) butter for bread rounds (⅛ teaspoon per round)

Cut out bread rounds with a 1¾-inch (4½-centimeter) cutter. Butter them.

Chop the mushrooms and sauté in 1 tablespoon of butter for 5 minutes. Add to the ingredients in the basic recipe along with the nutmeg. Heap on the prepared rounds. Decorate with any of the garnishes mentioned. Freeze on a cooky sheet. When frozen, put the canapés in freezer bags, label, and freeze. *Makes about 35 canapés. Storage time: 2 to 3 weeks.*

To use: Take canapés from the freezer and remove carefully from the bags. Arrange on a serving platter and cover with very damp paper towels. Thaw at room temperature for 1½ to 2 hours. Remove the paper towels and serve.

CURRIED CHICKEN CANAPÉS

1 loaf of white bread
1 ounce (30 grams) soft butter for bread rounds (⅛ teaspoon
    per round)
6 ounces (180 grams) cream cheese
few drops of onion juice
4 ounces (115 grams) cooked chicken, ground, or canned
    chicken spread
½ teaspoon curry powder
2 teaspoons minced chutney
1 tablespoon dairy sour cream
1 teaspoon lemon juice
1 tablespoon minced parsley

Cut out the bread rounds with a 1½-inch (4-centimeter) cutter or make them any shape you wish. Butter them.

Mash 4 ounces (115 grams) of the cream cheese. With a sharp knife, scrape the cut end of a small onion to extract a few drops of onion juice, and drop into the cheese. Add all other ingredients. Mix them well together so that the curry powder is well blended into the mixture. Heap on the prepared bread rounds. Put remaining 2 ounces (60 grams) cream cheese in a pastry tube and squeeze a small rosette on the top of each canapé. Or, if you do not want to be that fancy, just put a piece of parsley or a brandied raisin on top.

Place on a cooky sheet or whatever fits into your freezer space and freeze. When frozen, put the canapés in freezer bags, label, and return to the freezer. *Makes about 36 canapés.*

To use: Take from the freezer and remove canapés carefully (especially if you used parsley) from the bags. Place them on a serving platter and cover them with very damp paper towels. Thaw at room temperature for 1½ to 2 hours. Remove paper towels and serve.

CHICKEN CHUTNEY CANAPÉS

2¾ ounces (78 grams) silvered blanched almonds
7 ounces (198 grams) shredded coconut
1 loaf of Anadama bread
1½ ounces (45 grams) soft butter for rounds (⅛ teaspoon per
    round)
8 ounces (225 grams) cooked chicken, cubed
4 ounces (115 grams) cream cheese
1½ tablespoons minced chutney
1 teaspoon curry powder
2 tablespoons (30 milliliters) mayonnaise
½ teaspoon salt

These canapés are excellent served with Champagne, wine, tea, coffee or eggnog.

Toast the almonds in a preheated 400° F. (205° C.) oven until they are light brown. Toast the coconut until light brown. Watch it carefully!

Cut bread rounds with a 1½-inch (4-centimeter) cutter. Butter them.

Put the chicken through the finest blade of a meat grinder. Put it through again with the toasted almonds. Put this mixture in a bowl and add all other ingredients except coconut. Mix together thoroughly and heap on the prepared rounds. Sprinkle a little coconut on top and gently press it down to secure it. Freeze on a cooky sheet or whatever fits your freezer space. When frozen, put the canapés in freezer bags, label, and return to the freezer. *Makes about 30 canapés. Storage time: 2 weeks.*

To use: Take canapés from the freezer and carefully remove from the bags so you don't knock off the coconut. Arrange them on a serving platter and cover with very damp paper towels. Thaw at room temperature for 1½ to 2 hours. Remove paper towels and serve.

CHICKEN HAM CANAPÉS

2¾ ounces (78 grams) sliced blanched almonds
1 loaf of rye bread
2 ounces (60 grams) soft butter for bread rounds (⅛ teaspoon
    per round)
4 ounces (115 grams) canned chicken spread or ground cooked
    chicken
4 ounces (115 grams) canned ham spread or ground cooked
    ham
8 ounces (225 grams) cream cheese
1 tablespoon prepared mustard
1 ounce (30 milliliters) sherry
seasoned salt
3 tablespoons (45 milliliters) snipped chives

Put the almonds on a cooky sheet and into a 400° F. (205° C.)
oven. Let them take on a little color, but do not let them get really
brown or they will be bitter. Remove almonds and chop them
coarsely. Cool.

Cut out the bread rounds with a 1½-inch (4-centimeter) cutter,
or make them any shape you wish. Butter them.

With a fork, mash chicken and ham spreads and the cream
cheese. Add all other ingredients except the chives. Use seasoned
salt to taste. After the nuts have cooled, stir them into the cheese
mixture. Mix thoroughly. Heap on the prepared rounds. Sprinkle
the canapés liberally with chives, pressing them in gently so they
won't brush off when they are frozen. Freeze on a cooky sheet.
When frozen, put canapés in freezer bags, label, and return to the
freezer. *Makes about 60 canapés. Storage time: 2 weeks.*

To use: Take canapés from the freezer and carefully remove
them from the bags. Arrange them on a serving platter and cover
with very damp paper towels. Thaw at room temperature for 1½ to
2 hours. Remove paper towels and serve.

CHICKEN HAM TURNOVERS

1 recipe Chicken Ham Canapés (preceding recipe)
Flaky Pastry (see Index)
1 egg mixed with 1 teaspoon water

Use the recipe for Chicken Ham Canapés, but chop the almonds much finer.

Roll out the pastry ⅛ inch (½ centimeter) thick. Cut rounds with a 2⅛-inch (5½-centimeter) cutter, or use a glass or jar that size.

Put a little of the chicken-ham mixture on a pastry round, keeping it away from the edge. Moisten the edge with the egg mixture. Fold the rounds over to make half-moons and seal the edges firmly. Brush the tops with the egg mixture. Place the turnovers on a cooky sheet or whatever fits into your freezer space and freeze them. When frozen, remove the turnovers with a spatula and put them in a freezer bag, label, and return to the freezer. *Makes about 75 turnovers. Storage time: 1 month.*

You may take out as many turnovers as you need on any given occasion and simply put the remaining ones, still frozen, back in the freezer.

To use: With a sharp knife make a small slit in the top of each turnover. Bake the frozen turnovers on a cooky sheet, set inside another cooky sheet to keep them from browning too much on the bottom, in a 400° F. (205° C.) oven for 10 to 15 minutes, or until puffed and lightly browned.

CHICKEN PINWHEELS

1 ounce (30 grams) butter
1 medium-size onion, minced
8 ounces (225 grams) mushrooms, minced
8 ounces (225 grams) cooked chicken, ground
4 ounces (115 grams) cream cheese
2 tablespoons (30 milliliters) mayonnaise
1 tablespoon sherry
pinch of grated nutmeg
salt and pepper
Blue Cheese Pastry I (see Index)

Melt butter and sauté onion and mushrooms until tender. Cool. Mix them and all other ingredients except pastry together. Use seasoning to taste. Roll out the pastry to a rectangle 8 x 18 inches (20 x 45 centimeters), and spread the chicken mixture on it. Keep the mixture about ½ inch (1½ centimeters) away from one of the long edges. Roll the other long edge toward the one that is clear of filling. One way to do this is to roll out the ball of dough on a large sheet of wax paper to the proper dimensions. Then, after spreading it with the chicken mixture, it is easy to pick up the long edge of the paper and roll the dough away from you. Remember that you want a small neat canapé so the roll must not get too fat. Chill the roll in the wax paper for 2 hours until it is very firm. Cut the roll into ¼-inch (¾-centimeter) slices and freeze on a cooky sheet or whatever fits into your freezer space. When frozen, put the pinwheels in freezer bags,

label, and return to the freezer. *Makes 60 to 70 pinwheels. Storage time: 1 month.*

To use: Put the frozen pinwheels on a buttered cooky sheet with a raised edge. Set this inside another sheet to keep the pinwheels from scorching on the bottom. Bake the pinwheels in a preheated 400° F. (205° C.) oven for 10 to 12 minutes, or until puffy and golden. Watch them carefully.

CHICKEN LIVER CANAPÉS

1 loaf of white bread
2 ounces (60 grams) soft butter for the bread rounds (⅛ teaspoon per round)
2 onions, minced
3 ounces (90 grams) butter
1 pound (450 grams) chicken livers
3 ounces plus 1 teaspoon (100 milliliters) sherry
¼ teaspoon dried thyme
1 tablespoon minced parsley
salt and ground pepper
8 ounces (225 grams) cream cheese, softened

Cut out bread rounds with a 1½-inch (4-centimeter) cutter. Butter them.

Sauté onions in 3 ounces butter until lightly browned. Remove to a bowl. Put chicken livers in the same pan the onions were cooked in and sauté them until they are just done. Put them through the finest blade of a meat grinder and put them in the bowl with the onions. Pour 3 ounces of the sherry into the pan, and over low heat scrape up all the brown bits. Add this to the livers and onion. Add the thyme, parsley, and salt and pepper to taste. Mix thoroughly and spread on the prepared bread rounds.

Add the additional teaspoon of sherry to the softened cream cheese and mix well. With a pastry bag or tube, pipe the cheese around the edge of the canapés in a decorative fashion.

Freeze on a cooky sheet. When frozen, put the canapés in freezer bags, label, and return to the freezer. *Makes about 60 canapés. Storage time: 2 weeks.*

To use: Take canapés from the freezer and arrange them on a serving platter. Cover with very damp paper towels. Thaw at room temperature for 1½ to 2 hours. Remove the paper towels and serve.

CHICKEN LIVER PÂTÉ WITH APPLE

1 loaf of rye bread
1 medium-size onion, minced
2 apples, peeled, cored and minced
4 ounces (115 grams) butter
1 pound (450 grams) chicken livers
1 teaspoon salt
2 teaspoons Worcestershire sauce
1 teaspoon grated lemon rind

This spread may be served cold or hot.

To serve hot (which is the way I prefer it), make the toast rounds first. Cut the bread into 1¾-inch (4½-centimeter) rounds or whatever shape you choose. Put them on a cooky sheet and into a 350° F. (180° C.) oven for 5 or 6 minutes. They should feel dry to the touch but should not take on any color as they will be baked again later on. Remove the rounds and cover with a dry towel. Cool.

Sauté the onion and apples in 1 ounce of the butter until golden and tender. Set aside. Put the livers in salted boiling water, to cover. Bring again to a boil and simmer for no longer than 4 minutes. Drain them and put them in a blender. Add the salt, Worcestershire sauce and grated lemon rind. Melt remaining butter and pour into the blender. Blend at high speed until no lumps remain. Remove to a bowl and add the onion-apple mixture. Stir until well mixed. Spread the mixture on the prepared toast rounds. Freeze the canapés on a cooky sheet or whatever fits into your freezer space. When frozen, put the canapés in freezer bags, label, and return to the freezer. *Makes 30 to 36 canapés. Storage time: 2 weeks.*

To use: Place on a cooky sheet and into a 400° F. (205° C.) oven for 10 minutes, or until brown and bubbly.

To serve cold as a pâté: Put the liver-apple mixture in a 1-quart (1-liter) freezer container, label, and freeze. *Serves 6 to 8 people.*

To use: Thaw the spread in the container in the refrigerator for 24 hours. Put on a serving platter and mold it into a pretty shape. Surround with crackers.

CHICKEN LIVER PÂTÉ WITH BRANDIED RAISINS

4 slices of bacon
2 onions, chopped
2 pounds (900 grams) chicken livers
½ teaspoon dried thyme
1 bay leaf
salt and pepper
1 cup (¼ liter) Brandied Raisins (see Index)
2 ounces (60 milliliters) sherry
4 ounces (115 grams) butter, softened
parsley, minced
1 hard-cooked egg yolk

Fry bacon and reserve. Add chopped onions to the bacon fat in the pan and brown them. Remove the onions and reserve. Add livers, thyme, bay leaf, and salt and pepper to taste to the same pan, and sauté until the livers are slightly brown and just barely cooked. Discard bay leaf. Put the livers, onions and raisins twice through the finest blade of a meat grinder. Return the mixture to the pan with the sherry and move it around to collect the brown bits clinging to the pan. Mix to a very smooth paste. Add butter and mix well. If the pâté should seem at all dry, add a little more butter or sherry. Put in two 1-quart (1-liter) freezer containers, label, and freeze. *Serves 15 to 20 people. Storage time: 2 weeks.*

To use: Have some finely chopped parsley and/or a hard-cooked egg yolk ready to decorate the pâté.

Remove the pâté from the freezer 24 hours before you need it. Put it in the refrigerator, still in the containers, to thaw. When thawed, put the pâté on a serving platter, flatten it, and pat it into an oval. Score it with the tines of a fork and sprinkle it with the parsley. Or grate the hard-cooked egg yolk over the center part of the oval, and put a rim of finely chopped parsley around the edge. Serve with crackers a little on the sweet side.

MEATS

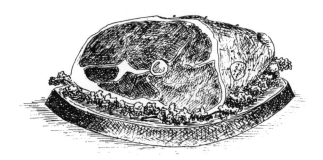

I've been married for seven interesting years to a wonderful man who used to raise Black Angus cattle. He loved those cattle so much that it took an exasperated family or a famine in the land for him ever to part with one and transfer it from pasture to freezer.

On our honeymoon, we spent a lot of time in his huge old barn in Massachusetts cutting up meat from a prime beef cow. We had been told that the cow might have swallowed a piece of wire and maybe contracted "hardware disease." Not knowing for sure what was wrong with her, and entertaining the possibility of a virus, the veterinarian had given her some shots of penicillin. Because of the use of penicillin, the vet admonished us that we should not eat the meat as it might affect the efficacy of the drug in our systems in time of need. For one whole year, two black Labrador Retrievers (his) and two Chesapeake Bay Retrievers (mine) dined on the choicest steaks and roasts while we ate supermarket offerings!

When we moved back to Maine, my husband sorrowfully left his small herd behind in the care of one of his sons. He reasoned that it would take too many years to turn our Maine pasture into a decent grazing meadow. Up here our fields are called "bee pastures" because they contain many more flowers than grass.

Before we came back, one twenty-year-old *grand dame* of the herd was so ancient she had to be sent to the abbatoir. My husband had not been able to part with her, as she had become "part of the family," and she would never become familiar with the inside of our freezer.

Not having any more of our own cattle, we have to be content with the store Braunschweiger, bologna and salami. I hope that they come from some other twenty-year-old girl who has had the same tender loving care that my husband's cows did.

LIVER CANAPÉS I

1 loaf of whole-wheat bread
1½ ounces (45 grams) soft butter for the rounds (⅛ teaspoon per round)
5 ounces (140 grams) canned liver paste
2 tablespoons minced green pepper (30 milliliters)
1 tablespoon mayonnaise
3 ounces (90 grams) cream cheese
2 ounces (60 grams) flat anchovy fillets

Cut the bread rounds with a 1½-inch (4-centimeter) cutter. Butter them.

Mash the liver paste. Add the green pepper and the mayonnaise to the liver paste. Mix thoroughly and spread on the prepared rounds. With a pastry bag or tube, pipe a line of softened cream cheese across the middle. Place a very thin strip of anchovy on it, pressing it down slightly. Freeze on a cooky sheet or whatever fits in your freezer space. When frozen, put the canapés in freezer bags, label, and return to the freezer. *Makes about 36 canapés. Storage time: 2 weeks.*

To use: Place frozen hors-d'oeuvre on a serving platter and cover with very damp paper towels. Thaw at room temperature for 1½ to 2 hours. Remove paper towels and serve.

LIVER CANAPÉS II

1 loaf of white bread
1 ounce (30 grams) soft butter for the rounds (⅛ teaspoon per
   round)
5 ounces (140 grams) canned liver paste
1 ounce (30 milliliters) sherry
4 ounces (115 grams) whole pimientos
3 ounces (90 grams) cream cheese
2 ounces (60 grams) flat anchovy fillets

Cut the bread rounds with a 1½-inch (4-centimeter) cutter. Butter them.

Mix liver paste and sherry. Spread the prepared rounds with the mixture. Cut pimientos into ¾-inch (2-centimeter) strips and wipe dry. Press a pimiento strip into the paste on each round and trim away any that hangs over the edge of the round. Fill a pastry bag or tube with the cream cheese and pipe a fluted line across the pimiento from one edge of the round to the other. Place a very thin strip of anchovy on the cream cheese. Freeze the canapés on a cooky sheet or whatever fits into your freezer space. When frozen, put the canapés in freezer bags, label, and return to the freezer. *Makes about 24 canapés. Storage time: 2 weeks.*

To use: Place the frozen hors-d'oeuvre on a serving platter and cover with very damp paper towels. Thaw at room temperature for 1½ to 2 hours. Remove paper towels and serve.

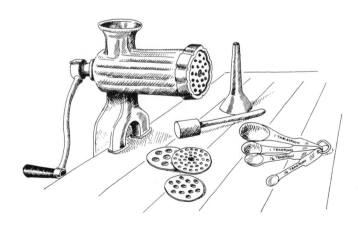

LIVER SAUSAGE SPREAD OR DIP

1 loaf of rye bread
4 ounces (115 grams) butter for rounds (⅛ teaspoon per
    round)
1 pound (450 grams) cream cheese
8 ounces (225 grams) Braunschweiger liver sausage
1 tablespoon prepared horseradish, drained
1½ tablespoons anchovy paste
1½ tablespoons grated onion
½ cup (1 deciliter) mayonnaise
1 tablespoon prepared mustard
sweet cream
kosher dill pickles

Cut bread rounds with a 1½-inch (4-centimeter) cutter. Butter them.

To use the spread: Mash the cream cheese and the Braunschweiger. Add the horseradish, anchovy paste, grated onion, mayonnaise and mustard. With a pastry bag and a large star tip with a ½-inch (1½-centimeter) opening, press a rosette of the mixture on the prepared rounds. Or, if you prefer, spread the rounds with a butter spreader.

Cut the dill pickles into ⅛-inch (½-centimeter) slices, then cut 4 edges off each slice all the way around. Press one of the cut-off pieces on the rosette, skin side up. Place the canapés on a cooky sheet or whatever fits into your freezer space, and freeze. When frozen, put the canapés in freezer bags, label, and return to the freezer. *Makes 100 canapés. Storage time: 2 weeks.*

To use: Place frozen hors-d'oeuvre on a serving platter and cover with very damp paper towels. Thaw at room temperature for 1½ to 2 hours. Remove paper towels and serve.

To use the dip: Mince 2 dill pickles (or more, depending on your fondness for them). Add to the Braunschweiger mixture. Put the dip in 1-quart (1-liter) freezer containers, label, and freeze. *Makes enough dip for 25 people.*

To use: Thaw in the freezer containers in the refrigerator for 24 hours. Whip thawed dip with a fork or wire whisk. Add a little sweet cream or dairy sour cream to give it the right dipping consistency. Place dip in a serving bowl. Surround the bowl with small rounds of rye or pumpernickel bread or toast.

LIVER PÂTÉ CANAPÉS WITH ALMONDS

1 loaf of Anadama or oatmeal bread
1½ ounces (45 grams) soft butter for the rounds (⅛ teaspoon
    per round)
2 ounces (60 grams) slivered blanched almonds, chopped
2¾ ounces (78 grams) slivered blanched almonds, for garnish
5 ounces (140 grams) canned liver paste
1 ounce (30 grams) soft butter
3 ounces (90 grams) cream cheese
1 tablespoon chili sauce
2 tablespoons (30 milliliters) snipped chives
1 ounce (30 milliliters) sherry
pinch of dried thyme
salt

This spread can be frozen in a 1-quart (1-liter) freezer container to be spread on the rounds another day.

Cut the bread rounds with a 1½-inch (4-centimeter) cutter. Butter them.

Toast the chopped slivered almonds and the slivered almonds for garnish. Put them on separate cooky sheets and into a 400° F. (205° C.) oven until they are golden. Do not get them too dark. Remove from the oven and cool.

Mix everything together except the slivered almonds for garnish. Use salt to taste. Spread thickly on the prepared rounds. Top with a slivered almond. Freeze the canapés on a cooky sheet or whatever fits into your freezer space. When frozen, put the canapés in freezer bags, label, and return to the freezer. *Makes about 36 canapés. Storage time: 2 weeks.*

To use: Remove canapés from the freezer and put them on a serving platter. Cover with very damp paper towels. Thaw at room temperature for 1½ to 2 hours. Remove paper towels and serve.

To freeze as a spread: Mix together all the ingredients except the almonds for garnish. Put the mixture in a 1-quart (1-liter) freezer container and put the extra almonds in a smaller container. Label and freeze both.

To use: Remove the containers of liver pâté and almonds from the freezer 24 hours before needed. Thaw in the refrigerator. Whip the pâté mixture with a fork and mold into a pleasing shape on a serving platter. Decorate with the toasted almonds and surround with interesting crackers. *Serves 8 to 10 people.*

LIVERWURST WITH RUM-SOAKED RAISINS

 1 tablespoon minced raisins
 1 ounce (30 milliliters) dark rum
 1 loaf of Anadama bread
 2 to 2½ ounces (60 to 75 grams) softened butter for rounds (⅛
     teaspoon per round)
 8 ounces (225 grams) liverwurst
 8 ounces (225 grams) cream cheese, softened
 2 tablespoons (30 milliliters) mayonnaise
 2 tablespoons (30 milliliters) snipped chives
 1 tablespoon prepared mustard
 parsley

This spread can be frozen in a 1-quart (1-liter) container to be spread on the rounds another day.

Soak the raisins in the rum for several hours.

Cut out the bread rounds with a 1½-inch (4-centimeter) cutter. Butter them.

Mash the liverwurst and cheese until well blended. Add the other ingredients including the rum-soaked minced raisins and the rum, but not the parsley. Mix thoroughly and spread on the prepared rounds. Decorate with parsley. Freeze the canapés on a cooky sheet or whatever fits into your freezer space. When frozen, put the canapés in freezer bags, label, and return to the freezer. *Makes 50 to 60 canapés. Storage time: 2 weeks.*

To use: Place the frozen hors-d'oeuvre on a serving platter, being careful not to break off the parsley as you take them from the bags. Cover them with very damp paper towels. Thaw at room temperature for 1½ to 2 hours. Remove paper towels and serve.

To freeze as a spread: Freeze the mixture in a 1-quart (1-liter) container.

To use: Thaw in the refrigerator for 24 hours. Place on a serving platter and shape into a roll. Surround with crackers. *Serves 6 to 8 people.*

JANE'S PARTY PÂTÉ

1 envelope (7 grams) unflavored gelatin
10½ ounces (298 grams) beef consommé
8 ounces (225 grams) cream cheese
4¼ ounces (123 grams) canned liver paste
4½ ounces (130 grams) canned deviled ham
2 tablespoons minced parsley
1½ ounces (45 milliliters) sherry
2 tablespoons (30 milliliters) prepared mustard
2 tablespoons (30 milliliters) Worcestershire sauce
½ teaspoon dried thyme
2 tablespoons (30 milliliters) snipped chives
watercress or parsley for garnish

Soften gelatin in ½ cup (1 deciliter) consommé for 5 minutes. Bring the rest of the consommé to a boil and dissolve the softened gelatin in it. Cool. Mash the cheese, liver paste and deviled ham together with a fork. Add the other ingredients except garnish greens, but including the consommé with the gelatin. Mix well with a wire whisk. Chill pâté in the refrigerator until it just begins to set. Stir gently and pour into a 1-quart (1-liter) mold, lightly oiled with vegetable oil. Chill until firm. Put foil over the top and secure it with freezer tape. Label and freeze. *Serves 20 to 30 people. Storage time: 1 month.*

To use: Remove pâté from the freezer and thaw in the refrigerator for 24 hours. Unmold and decorate with the greens. Serve with interesting crackers or Patty's Melba Toast (see Index).

HOT LIVER PÂTÉ CANAPÉS WITH ORANGE

1 loaf of white bread
2 ounces (60 grams) slivered blanched almonds, chopped
3 ounces (90 grams) cream cheese
5 ounces (140 grams) canned liver paste
1 ounce (30 milliliters) brandy
1 tablespoon grated orange rind
1 tablespoon chopped parsley

This spread can be frozen in a 1-quart (1-liter) freezer container to be spread on rounds another day.

Cut the bread rounds with a 1¾-inch (4½-centimeter) cutter, or any shape you wish. Put them on a cooky sheet and into a 350° F. (180° C.) oven for 5 to 6 minutes. They should be a little dry to the touch but should not take on any color as they will be baked later on.

Put the chopped almonds on a cooky sheet and into a 400° F. (205° C.) oven. Stir and check them often as you do not want them too dark or they will be bitter. Take them out when they are a deep golden color. Cool.

Soften the cream cheese and mix thoroughly with all other ingredients. Heap on the toast rounds and freeze on a cooky sheet or whatever fits your freezer space. When frozen, put the canapés in freezer bags, label, and return to the freezer. *Makes about 40 canapés. Storage time: 2 weeks.*

To use: Bake the frozen canapés on a cooky sheet in a 400° F. (205° C.) oven for 10 to 12 minutes.

DRIED-BEEF CANAPÉS

    1 loaf of rye or whole-wheat bread
    4 ounces (115 grams) dried beef
    2 ounces (60 grams) shelled walnuts
    5 ounces (140 grams) Cheddar cheese, grated
    3 ounces (90 grams) cream cheese
    ¼ teaspoon chili powder
    2 tablespoons (30 milliliters) tomato paste
    1 tablespoon snipped chives

Cut out the bread rounds with a 1½-inch (4-centimeter) cutter or any shape you wish. Put them on a cooky sheet and into a 350° F. (180° C.) oven for 5 to 6 minutes. They should be a little dry to the touch but should not take on any color as they will be baked later on. Remove from the oven and cool.

Put the dried beef in a strainer and pour hot water over it to remove excess salt. Spread out some paper towels and put the beef on them. Roll up the towels and squeeze the water out of the beef. Put beef and walnuts through the finest blade of a meat grinder. Mash Cheddar and cream cheeses. Mix all the ingredients together until well blended. Heap on the prepared toast rounds. Freeze on a cooky sheet or whatever fits your freezer space. When frozen, put the canapés in freezer bags, label, and return to the freezer. *Makes about 40 canapés. Storage time: 3 weeks.*

To use: Put the frozen canapés on a cooky sheet and bake in a 400° F. (205° C.) oven until heated through and bubbly, about 10 minutes.

DRIED-BEEF ROLL

SPONGE ROLL:

> 1 to 2 teaspoons flour for the pan
> 6 eggs
> 1 cup (140 grams) sifted unbleached flour
> 4 ounces (115 grams) Parmesan cheese, grated

Line a buttered jelly-roll pan 10 × 15 inches (25 × 38 centimeters) with a raised edge, with wax paper. Butter the paper also and flour it with the teaspoon of flour. Put the flour on the wax paper and shake it around, then turn the pan upside down to get rid of any excess flour.

Beat the eggs in the top part of a nonaluminum 2-quart (2-liter) double boiler, over simmering water and low heat, until they are very thick. Keep beating until the eggs have tripled in volume, 8 to 10 minutes. Pour eggs quickly into a large bowl and continue beating until the eggs have cooled to lukewarm. Sift the 1 cup flour over the eggs and, with a large spoon, quickly and carefully fold it in. Pour the mixture into the prepared jelly-roll pan and tip the pan in all directions to spread the mixture evenly. Sprinkle the Parmesan cheese on top. Bake in preheated oven 350° F. (180° C.) for 12 minutes. It should just be beginning to take on a little color; when pressed with a finger, the sponge should spring back.

Turn sponge roll out on a large sheet of wax paper. Working as quickly as you can, remove the paper from the bottom of the sponge and cut the sponge into halves across the middle. Cut the crusty edges off. Spread out another piece of wax paper and put one of the halves on it. Roll it up from the long edge with the wax paper rolled right up in it. Roll as tightly as you can so the roll will not be too big around when it is filled. Do the same with the other half. Cover both rolls with a clean tea towel and allow to cool at room temperature.

Unroll them carefully, remove wax paper, and spread with the beef filling.

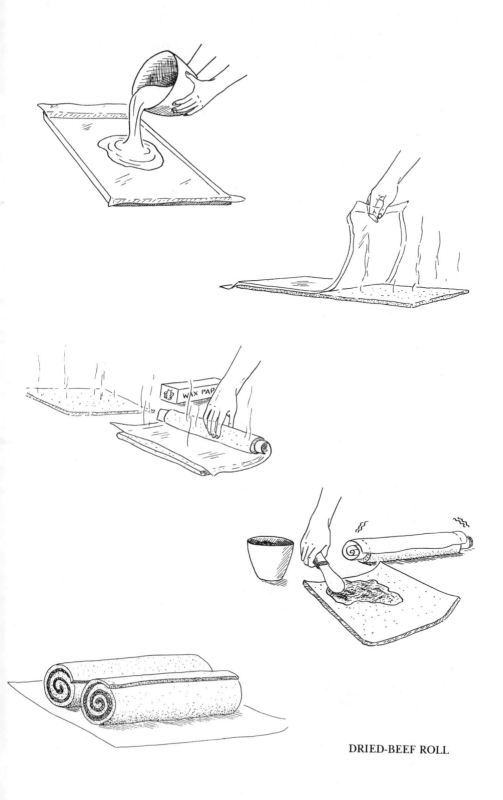

DRIED-BEEF ROLL

DRIED-BEEF FILLING:

> 6 ounces (170 grams) unsalted butter
> 6 ounces (170 grams) cream cheese
> 5 ounces (140 grams) dried beef, minced
> 1 teaspoon Worcestershire sauce
> 1 ounce (30 milliliters) sherry
> 3 tablespoons (45 milliliters) snipped chives

Soften the butter and the cheese. Mix well with all the other ingredients. Spread on the sponges and roll up. Wrap rolls in wax paper and chill until firm. Cut into ½-inch (1½-centimeter) slices and freeze on a cooky sheet or whatever fits into your freezer space. When frozen, put the beef rolls in freezer bags, label, and return to the freezer. *Makes 36 canapés.*

To use: Remove beef rolls from the freezer bags and arrange on a serving platter. Cover with very damp paper towels. Thaw at room temperature for 2 hours. Remove paper towels and serve.

VARIATION I
(CHICKEN FILLING):

> 8 ounces (225 grams) cream cheese
> 8 ounces (225 grams) cooked chicken, minced
> ½ cup (1 deciliter) mayonnaise
> ½ cup (1 deciliter) minced parsley
> 2½ tablespoons (38 milliliters) minced capers
> ½ cup (1 deciliter) minced celery
> ½ teaspoon salt
> ground pepper

Make the sponge as described in the basic recipe. Mash the cream cheese with a fork and add all other ingredients. Mix until everything is well blended. Spread filling on the prepared sponge rolls. Roll up and freeze as directed.

VARIATION II
(SHRIMP FILLING):

> 8 ounces (225 grams) cream cheese
> 8 ounces (225 grams) cooked shrimps, shelled and minced (10 to 12 large shrimps)

½ cup (1 deciliter) minced parsley
½ cup (1 deciliter) minced celery
2 tablespoons (30 milliliters) chili sauce
2 tablespoons (30 milliliters) finely chopped sweet pickle
1 teaspoon dried dillweed
½ teaspoon dried tarragon

Make the sponge as described in the basic recipe. Mash the cream cheese with a fork and add all other ingredients. Mix until everything is well blended. Spread filling on the prepared sponge rolls. Roll up and freeze as directed.

SAVORY MEATBALLS

1½ pounds (675 grams) lean ground beef
2 tablespoons (30 milliliters) minced celery
2 tablespoons (30 milliliters) minced onion
2 tablespoons (30 milliliters) minced green pepper
8 saltines, crumbled
1 egg, beaten
¼ teaspoon garlic powder
¼ to ½ cup (½ to 1 deciliter) water
1½ ounces (45 grams) butter
Savory Sauce (see Index)

Mix together all ingredients except butter and sauce, using only as much of the water as needed to be able to shape the meat into firm little balls that will hold their shape. Roll them between the palms of your hands into grape-size balls. Melt the butter over medium heat, and sauté the balls until they start to brown. Do only a few at a time or they won't brown properly. Remove them as they brown and cool them. When cold, put them on a cooky sheet or whatever fits into your freezer space and freeze. When frozen, put the meatballs in freezer bags, label, and return to the freezer. *Makes 40 to 50 balls. Storage time: 1 month.*

To use: Place the frozen meatballs on a buttered cooky sheet with a raised edge. Bake in a 400° F. (205° C.) oven for 8 to 10 minutes, or until heated through.

Put a bowl of Savory Sauce on a platter and surround it with the meatballs. Have cocktail picks handy.

JUNIPER HILL MEAT PUFFS AND PINWHEELS

1 ounce (30 grams) butter
4 ounces (115 grams) minced onion
4 ounces (115 grams) lean ground beef
⅓ cup (½ deciliter) dairy sour cream
2 ounces (60 grams) blue cheese, grated
1 teaspoon A.1. Sauce
½ teaspoon salt
ground pepper
Blue Cheese Pastry II (see Index)

Melt butter in a frying pan and sauté the onion until starting to brown on the edges. Push to one side of the pan and brown the beef, breaking up the meat as you do so. Off the heat, add all other ingredients. Use pepper to taste. Mix well and cool thoroughly.

Make the pastry and roll out to a sheet ⅛ inch (½ centimeter) thick. Cut into 1½-inch (4-centimeter) rounds. Dip your finger in cold water and wet the edge of a round. Put about ½ teaspoon of the mixture in the center of the round. Place a second round on the first one, stretching it to fit over the filling. Press the edges together firmly with floured fork tines.

Place the puffs on a cooky sheet or whatever fits into your freezer space. Freeze. When frozen, put the puffs in freezer bags, label, and return to the freezer. *Makes about 40 puffs. Storage time: 2 months.*

To use: With a sharp knife, make a small hole or slit in the top of each frozen puff. Bake on a cooky sheet in a 400° F. (205° C.) oven for 10 to 15 minutes. They should be puffed and golden. Put a second cooky sheet under the first, setting one inside the other, to keep the bottoms of the puffs from getting too brown. Every oven is different and this may not be necessary for you.

To make pinwheels: Take the scraps of dough left over and press them gently together. Chill in the refrigerator for another hour. Roll out to a rectangle 10 × 5 inches (25 × 13 centimeters). Spread the rest of the meat mixture on it, keeping it away from one of the long edges. Roll the other long edge toward the one that is clear of filling. Wet the clear edge and seal to the roll by pressing it with your fingers. Wrap in wax paper and return to the refrigerator. When thoroughly chilled, cut the roll into ½-inch (1½-centimeter) slices.

Makes 16 additional pastries. Freeze with the puffs and bake as you bake the puffs.

CORNED-BEEF PINWHEELS

2½ ounces (71 grams) sliced corned beef
6 ounces (170 grams) cream cheese
5 ounces (140 grams) canned deviled ham
1 tablespoon prepared mustard
2 tablespoons (30 milliliters) minced dill pickle
1 tablespoon minced parsley
1 teaspoon grated onion

Carefully open the corned-beef slices. Mash the cheese and add all other ingredients except the corned beef. Mix thoroughly and spread on the beef slices. Roll up and chill in the refrigerator until very firm. Cut rolls with a very sharp knife into 1-inch (2½-centimeter) pieces, to make 4 little rolls per slice of corned beef. Freeze on a cooky sheet or whatever fits into your freezer space. When frozen, put the pinwheels in freezer bags, label, and return to the freezer. *Makes 48 pinwheels. Storage time: 2 weeks.*

To use: Take pinwheels from the bags and arrange them on a serving platter. Cover with plastic wrap and thaw in the refrigerator for 24 hours.
NOTE: The packaged corned beef I buy has 4-inch-square (10-centimeter) slices. If your slices are larger or smaller, you will cut more or fewer pieces accordingly.

CORNED-BEEF CANAPÉS

1 loaf of rye bread
2 ounces (60 grams) Cheddar cheese
2 ounces (60 grams) cream cheese
4½ ounces (130 grams) canned corned beef spread or cooked
   corned beef, ground
1 tablespoon chili sauce
2 tablespoons (30 milliliters) minced dill pickle
2 teaspoons prepared mustard

Cut out bread rounds with a 1¾-inch (4½-centimeter) cutter.

Put them on a cooky sheet and into a 350° F. (180° C.) oven for 5 to 6 minutes. They should be a little dry to the touch but should not take on any color as they will be baked later on. Remove the rounds and cover with a dry towel. Allow them to cool.

Grate the Cheddar cheese and mash the cream cheese. Mix them together and add all other ingredients. When well blended, heap on the prepared rye toast rounds. Freeze the canapés on a cooky sheet or whatever fits well into your freezer space. When frozen, put the canapés in freezer bags, label, and return to the freezer. *Makes about 50 canapés. Storage time: 1 month.*

To use: Bake the frozen canapés in a 400° F. (205° C.) oven for 8 to 10 minutes.

HAM POTATO BALLS

4½ ounces (130 grams) canned deviled ham or home-cooked
    ham, ground
1 cup (¼ liter) mashed potato
2 tablespoons (30 milliliters) minced dill pickle
1 teaspoon brown sugar
1 tablespoon vinegar
1 tablespoon minced parsley
½ teaspoon prepared mustard
garlic powder
2 cups (½ liter) fine dry bread crumbs
2 eggs, beaten
fat for deep frying

Mix all the ingredients together except the eggs, crumbs and fat for frying. Use garlic powder to taste. Chill for 1 hour. Shape into bite-size balls, about the size of a large grape. Roll them in the crumbs. Roll in beaten egg and then in the crumbs again. Put on wax paper and dry in the air for 1 hour. Heat the fat to 380° F. (194° C.). Put the ham potato balls in one layer in a frying basket and lower into the hot fat for 1 minute or less. Just watch them carefully and remove them when they are partially browned—a nice golden color. Drain on a piece of brown paper. Cool. Put them in freezer bags, label, and freeze. *Makes about 50 ham potato balls. Storage time: 1 month.*

To use: Take as many ham potato balls out of the freezer as you want for any given cocktail time and return the rest to the freezer.

Place on a cooky sheet and bake in a 350° F. (180° C.) oven until heated through. They have already been cooked and partially browned so all they need is 8 to 10 minutes in this moderate oven. Serve with cocktail picks and accompany with Sweet-Sour Sauce, Horseradish Cream or Mustard-Caper Sauce (see Index).

NOTE: This could have many variations, so get your imagination going. Substitute chicken for the ham, use minced mushrooms and sherry, other ground meats or most anything you can dream up. Have different kinds on the same platter. Experiment!

HAM CHUTNEY ROLLS

3 ounces (90 grams) cream cheese
1 ounce (30 grams) butter
½ teaspoon prepared mustard
2 teaspoons chopped chutney
1 tablespoon snipped chives
1 tablespoon finely chopped pecans
5 ounces (140 grams) cooked ham slices

Mash the cream cheese and add all other ingredients except the ham. Spread mixture generously on the ham slices. Roll them up, starting with the long side, and chill them until very firm. With a sharp knife slice to any desired thickness. I do not give an exact measurement here because it all depends on how tightly or loosely you roll them up. You should have a bite-size morsel that can be popped into the mouth in a single bite. Very good, too.

Freeze the rolls on a cooky sheet. When frozen, put them in freezer bags, label, and return to the freezer. *Makes 30 to 40 ham chutney rolls.*

To use: Thaw on a serving platter, covered tightly with plastic wrap, in the refrigerator for 5 to 6 hours.

NOTE: The packages of ham I use have 6 slices in them and each slice makes about 10 ham rolls, depending on how wide they are cut. You will need 3 or 4 ham slices for this amount of spread.

CURRIED HAM AND EGG SPREAD

2 hard-cooked egg yolks
5 ounces (140 grams) canned deviled ham or home-cooked
    ham, ground
2 ounces (60 grams) soft butter
2 ounces (60 grams) cream cheese
2 tablespoons (30 milliliters) chopped parsley
½ teaspoon curry powder
2 teaspoons minced chutney
1 tablespoon mayonnaise
2 hard-cooked egg yolks for garnish
1 to 2 tablespoons cream, if necessary
watercress, celery tops, etc., for garnish

Grate the first 2 hard-cooked egg yolks or mash with a fork. Add all the other ingredients except the cream and garnishes. Mix thoroughly and put in a 1-pint (½-liter) freezer container, label, and freeze. *Serves 6 to 8 people. Storage time: 2 weeks.*

Grate the 2 hard-cooked egg yolks for garnish and put them in a small freezer bag. Squeeze all the air out of the bag, label, and freeze.

To use: Thaw the container of spread and the bag of egg yolks in the refrigerator for 24 hours. Place the spread in a bowl and whip it with a wire whisk. Add a little of the cream if it seems too dry. Put the mixture on a serving platter and shape into a flattened oval. Sprinkle the grated yolks over the top and surround with pretty greens. Serve with Patty's Melba Toast (see Index).

HAM PINWHEELS

10 ounces (285 grams) packaged cooked ham slices, or home-
    cooked ham slices
2 teaspoons prepared mustard
⅛ teaspoon ground cloves
4 ounces (115 grams) cream cheese
2 tablespoons (30 milliliters) dairy sour cream
2 tablespoons (30 milliliters) minced parsley
Blue Cheese Pastry I (see Index)

Using the finest blade of a meat grinder, grind the ham. Put it in a bowl and add all other ingredients except pastry. Mix thoroughly.

Make the pastry. Roll it out on a floured surface to a rectangle ⅛ inch (½ centimeter) thick and roughly 14 x 20 inches (35 x 50 centimeters). Cut the pastry lengthwise into halves and move the halves a little apart. Spread half the ham mixture on half the pastry, keeping it ½ inch (1½ centimeters) away from one of the long edges. Start rolling the other long edge toward the one that is clear of the ham mixture, and roll it up jelly-roll fashion. Wet the long clear edge with water and press it gently to seal it. Wrap in wax paper and chill until firm. It makes for easier handling if you cut the long roll into halves with a very sharp knife before refrigerating. Roll up the other half in the same way.

When rolls are very firm, remove them and slice them into ¼-inch (¾-centimeter) slices. Freeze on a cooky sheet or whatever fits best in your freezer space. When frozen, put the pinwheels in freezer bags, label, and return to the freezer. *Makes about 50 pinwheels. Storage time: 3 weeks.*

To use: Bake the frozen pastries on a lightly buttered cooky sheet, set inside another cooky sheet, in a 400° F. (205° C.) oven for 10 to 12 minutes, until puffed and golden.

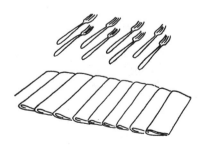

CURRIED HAM CANAPÉS

1 loaf of rye bread
4 ounces (115 grams) cooked ham
4 ounces (115 grams) Swiss cheese
4 ounces (115 grams) shelled pecans
2 tablespoons (30 milliliters) mayonnaise
½ teaspoon curry powder
1 ounce (30 milliliters) sherry
1 tablespoon minced parsley

Cut the bread rounds with a 1¾-inch (4½-centimeter) cutter, or any shape you wish. Put them on a cooky sheet and into a 350° F. (180° C.) oven. Leave them for 5 or 6 minutes. They should be a little dry to the touch but should not take on any color as they will be baked later on. Remove them from the oven, cover them with a dry towel, and allow them to cool.

Put the ham, Swiss cheese and pecans through the finest blade of a meat grinder. Add all other ingredients and mix thoroughly. Heap on the prepared rounds. Freeze the canapés on a cooky sheet or whatever fits into your freezer space. When frozen, put the canapés in freezer bags, label, and return to the freezer. *Makes about 36 canapés. Storage time: 2 weeks.*

To use: Bake in a 350° F. (180° C.) oven for 10 minutes, or until brown and bubbly.

HAM CANAPÉS WITH WALNUTS

1 loaf of rye bread
2 ounces (60 grams) soft butter for the bread rounds (⅛ teaspoon per round)
4 ounces (115 grams) liverwurst
4 ounces (115 grams) cream cheese
4 ounces (115 grams) cooked ham, ground
1 tablespoon grated onion
1 tablespoon snipped chives
2 ounces (60 grams) butter, softened
2 tablespoons (30 milliliters) chopped green pepper
2 teaspoons prepared mustard
4 ounces (115 grams) shelled walnut halves

Cut out the rounds with a 1½-inch (4-centimeter) cutter or any shape you wish. Butter them.

Mash the liverwurst and cream cheese together. Add the ground ham and all other ingredients except the walnuts. Heap the mixture on the prepared rye bread rounds and press a walnut half on the top of each one. Freeze on a cooky sheet or whatever fits into your freezer space. When frozen, put the canapés in freezer bags, label, and return to the freezer. *Makes about 50 canapés. Storage time: 2 weeks.*

To use: Remove canapés from freezer bags and arrange on a serving platter. Cover with very damp paper towels. Thaw at room temperature for 1½ to 2 hours. Remove paper towels and serve.

HAM-EGGPLANT CANAPÉS

1 loaf of rye bread
2 ounces (60 grams) soft butter for rounds (⅛ teaspoon per round)
8 ounces (225 grams) cream cheese
4 ounces (115 grams) canned ham spread or home-cooked ham, ground
4 ounces (115 grams) canned eggplant appetizer or your own Eggplant Caviar (see Index)
1 teaspoon Worcestershire sauce
1 tablespoon sherry
1 tablespoon chopped parsley
parsley, for garnish

This recipe can be frozen in a 1-quart (1-liter) container to be spread on the bread rounds another day.

Cut the bread into 1½-inch (4-centimeter) rounds with a cooky or canapé cutter, or make them any shape you wish. Butter them.

Mash the cream cheese and add all other ingredients except garnish. Mix thoroughly and spread on the prepared rye bread rounds. Press a sprig of parsley on top of each round. Freeze the canapés on a cooky sheet, or whatever fits into your freezer space. When frozen, put the canapés in a freezer bag, label, and return to the freezer. *Makes about 50 canapés. Storage time: 3 weeks.*

To use: Remove from the freezer and carefully take canapés out of the bag so you don't break the parsley. Put them on a serving platter and cover with very damp paper towels. Thaw at room temperature for 1½ to 2 hours. Remove paper towels and serve.

To use as a spread: After mixing all the ingredients together well, put the spread in a 1-quart (1-liter) container and freeze.

To use: Thaw the container in the refrigerator for 24 hours. Put on a serving platter and pat into any shape you may choose. Serve the molded pâté surrounded with rye Melba toast or rye crackers. *Serves 8 to 10 people.*

HAM OR TONGUE CANAPÉS

1 loaf of rye bread
1½ ounces (45 grams) soft butter for bread rounds (⅛ teaspoon per round)
4 ounces (115 grams) cooked ham or tongue, finely ground
1 ounce (30 milliliters) sherry
2 tablespoons (30 milliliters) minced parsley
5 ounces (140 grams) Swiss cheese
4 ounces (115 grams) cream cheese
4 ounces (115 grams) butter, softened
2 tablespoons (30 milliliters) prepared mustard

Cut out the bread rounds with a 1½-inch (4-centimeter) cutter, or whatever shape you wish. Butter them.

Grind the ham or tongue in a meat grinder and add the sherry and parsley. Cut the Swiss cheese into rounds the same size as the bread rounds. Spread the prepared bread rounds thickly with the cream cheese. Place a round of Swiss cheese on each one and press down to secure it. Mix the 4 ounces butter and the mustard well; with a pastry bag or tube, pipe mustard butter around the edge of the rounds. Fill the centers with the ground ham or tongue. Freeze the canapés on a cooky sheet or whatever fits into your freezer space. When frozen, put the canapés in freezer bags, label, and return to the freezer. *Makes about 36 canapés. Storage time: 3 weeks.*

To use: Put the frozen canapés on a serving platter and cover with very damp paper towels. Thaw at room temperature for 1½ to 2 hours. Remove paper towels and serve.

HAM AND CHICKEN ROLLS

4 ounces (115 grams) cooked chicken
2 ounces (60 grams) butter, softened
2 teaspoons prepared mustard
3 ounces (90 grams) cream cheese
⅛ teaspoon ground rosemary
1 tablespoon finely minced parsley
5 ounces (140 grams) packaged cooked ham slices or home-baked ham, sliced very thin

Put the chicken through the finest blade of a meat grinder. Add all other ingredients except the ham. Mix thoroughly. Spread the mixture on 4 ham slices and roll them up, starting on the long side. Wrap the rolls in plastic wrap and refrigerate until firm. With a sharp knife cut them to whatever length you want them. Use 1-inch (2¼-centimeter) rolls with cocktail picks and dip into a sauce of your choosing. Longer rolls can be picked up in the fingers and eaten as is. Freeze on a cooky sheet or whatever fits into your freezer space. When frozen, put the rolls in freezer bags, label, and return to the freezer. *Makes from 12 to 24 depending on how long you choose to make them. Storage time: 2 weeeks.*

To use: Remove rolls from the bags and place on a serving platter 24 hours before you will need them. Cover with very damp paper towels, then in plastic wrap. Thaw in the refrigerator.

SWEET-SOUR HAM BALLS

8 ounces (225 grams) cooked ham, ground
2 ounces (60 grams) shelled walnuts
¼ cup (½ deciliter) finely minced green olives
2 teaspoons prepared mustard
1 teaspoon Worcestershire sauce
½ cup (1 deciliter) finest bread crumbs
1 egg
Sweet-Sour Sauce (see Index)

Put the ham and walnuts through the finest blade of a meat grinder. Add all other ingredients except the Sweet-Sour Sauce.

Shape into grape-size balls by rolling the mixture in the palms of your hands. Freeze the balls on a cooky sheet or whatever fits into your freezer space. When frozen, put them in freezer bags, label, and return to the freezer. *Makes about 50 ham balls. Storage time: 2 weeks.*

To use: Take out as many ham balls as you want to use and put them on a cooky sheet or pie plate. Bake in a 350° F. (180° C.) oven for 15 minutes. Put a bowl of Sweet-Sour Sauce on a platter and surround it with the ham balls. Have cocktail picks available.

BACON ONION CANAPÉS

1 loaf of white bread
1 ounce (30 grams) butter
1 cup (¼ liter) minced onion
3 strips of raw bacon
4 ounces (115 grams) Cheddar cheese
⅛ teaspoon grated mace

Cut out bread rounds with a 1¾-inch (4½-centimeter) cutter. Put them on a cooky sheet and bake in a 350° F. (180° C.) oven for 5 or 6 minutes. They should get a little dry to the touch but should not take on any color as they will be baked again later on. Remove them and cover with a dry towel. Allow them to cool.

Sauté the onion in the butter until golden. Cool. Mince the raw bacon. Grate the cheese and add all the ingredients to it, including the onion and bacon. Mix well and pile lightly on the toast rounds. Freeze the canapés on a cooky sheet or whatever fits best in your freezer space. When frozen, put in freezer bags, label, and return to the freezer. *Makes about 40 canapés. Storage time: 2 weeks.*

To use: Bake the frozen canapés in a 400° F. (205° C) oven for 10 minutes, until lightly brown and bubbly, or broil under medium heat.

SALAMI WITH ORANGE BUTTER

1 loaf of rye bread
2 ounces (60 grams) soft butter for bread rounds (1 teaspoon
    per round)
4 ounces (115 grams) butter
grated rind of 1 orange
1 tablespoon orange juice
8 ounces (225 grams) salami slices
parsley

Cut rounds with a 1½-inch (4-centimeter) cutter. Butter them. It may seem unnecessary to butter the bread rounds when so much butter is in the spread but, unless you do, the moisture from the salami slices and orange juice will seep into the bread and make a soggy canapé when thawed.

Mix the 4 ounces butter, orange rind and juice. Spread on the prepared rounds. Cut salami with the same cutter used for bread rounds. Place a slice of salami on a round and press it down to secure it. With a pastry bag or tube, pipe a rosette of the same orange butter on top. Place a piece of parsley in the center of the rosette. The men in our group of friends seem to like this canapé a great deal. Freeze on a cooky sheet or whatever seems to fit into your freezer space. When frozen, put the canapés in freezer bags, label, and return to the freezer. *Makes about 30 canapés. Storage time: 1 to 2 weeks.*

To use: Place frozen hors-d'oeuvre on a serving platter and cover with very damp paper towels. Thaw at room temperature for 1½ to 2 hours. Remove paper towels and serve.

VARIATION:

Put the salami through the finest blade of a meat grinder. Mix it well with most of the orange butter and mound on the bread rounds. Top with a rosette of orange butter. Freeze and thaw as in the basic recipe.

SALAMI CANAPÉS

1 loaf of rye bread
1½ ounces (45 grams) soft butter for bread rounds (⅛ teaspoon per round)
6 ounces (180 grams) cream cheese
3 ounces (90 grams) blue cheese
¼ teaspoon dried dillweed
1 teaspoon grated onion
1 tablespoon brandy
1 tablespoon dark rum
4 ounces (115 grams) party salami (small slices)
mayonnaise
capers

Cut bread rounds with a 1½-inch (4-centimeter) cutter or any shape you wish. Butter them.

Mash both cheeses together and add the dill, onion, brandy and dark rum. Spread evenly on the prepared rounds. Cut the salami with the same cutter and press into the cheese spread. With a pastry bag or tube, put a rosette of mayonnaise on each salami slice. Place a single caper in each rosette. Freeze on a cooky sheet or whatever fits into your freezer space. When frozen, put the canapés in freezer bags, label, and return to the freezer. *Makes about 30 canapés. Storage time: 1 to 2 weeks.*

To use: Place frozen hors-d'oeuvre on a serving platter and cover with very damp paper towels. Thaw at room temperature for 1½ to 2 hours. Remove paper towels and serve.

SAUSAGE AND GREEN-PEPPER PATTIES

30 uncooked Patty Shells (see Index)
1 loaf of white bread
8 ounces (225 grams) fresh sausage meat
1 teaspoon butter
1 onion, minced
3 tablespoons (45 milliliters) minced green pepper (half of 1
    pepper)
1 tablespoon tomato paste
1 small egg, slightly beaten
pinch of dried thyme
salt

Make the patty shells according to the directions in that recipe.
Cover with plastic wrap while you prepare the filling.

Sauté the sausage meat in 1 teaspoon butter over low heat until
lightly browned and cooked through. Remove to a bowl with a slotted spoon and mash with a fork until there are no lumps. Put
minced onion and green pepper in the same pan the sausage was
cooked in and sauté until they are golden and tender, adding more
butter if necessary. Add to the sausage. Add the tomato paste, egg
and thyme. Taste for salt as sausage meat varies a lot. When cooled,
put the mixture by ½ teaspoons in the center of the patty shells.
Be careful not to get any on the rims. Freeze the filled shells on a
cooky sheet or whatever fits best into your freezer space. When
frozen, put the shells in freezer bags, label, and return to the
freezer. *Makes 30 filled patty shells. Storage time: 2 weeks.*

To use: Place the frozen patties on a cooky sheet set inside another cooky sheet and bake in a 400° F. (205° C.) oven for about 10
minutes, or until the sides have risen up around the sausage and the
patties are golden and puffed. The second cooky sheet keeps them
from browning too fast on the bottom.

To make canapés: There will be sausage and green-pepper filling left over after filling the pastries, so you can use it to spread on
some toast rounds.

Make the toast rounds by cutting the white bread slices with a
1¾-inch (4½-centimeter) cutter, or make them any shape you wish.
Put them on a cooky sheet and bake in a 350° F. (180° C.) oven for 5
to 6 minutes. They should be a little dry to the touch but should not

take on any color as they will be baked later on. Remove and cool, covered with a dry towel.

Put the remaining sausage and green-pepper mixture on the toast rounds. Freeze them the same as the pastries.

To use: Bake canapés in a 400 F. (205° C.) oven for 8 to 10 minutes, or until heated through and brown and bubbly. Bake the pastries first; when they are done, put in the toast rounds.

VEGETABLES

Our large vegetable garden really keeps my husband and me hopping in the summer to try and stay ahead of the pigweed and purslane which can be controlled only by getting down and crawling around on all fours. It produces aching backs, dirty torn fingernails, dampened brows and delicious vegetables.

There are many good canapés to have in the deep freeze, but in the summer a most welcome sight at a party is a platter of fresh vegetables, with a bowl of Rémoulade Sauce to dip them into. It is pretty and refreshing and generally appreciated on a hot day.

Sauces can be kept in the freezer in small containers. With a few hours notice you can thaw as many as you might need for your cocktail guests. It takes 3 to 4 hours for a ½-pint (¼-liter) container of sauce to thaw at room temperature. Keep some celery, carrots, zucchini slices, cauliflowerets, cucumber spears or kohlrabi slices in a plastic bag in the refrigerator during the hot months and you will be ready for any emergency.

Eggplant Caviar is very freezable and great to have on hand to use by itself or in combination with other ingredients. Every book has a recipe for it but I've included mine anyway.

ARTICHOKE CANAPÉS

1 loaf of Anadama or white bread
1½ ounces (45 grams) soft butter for bread rounds (⅛ teaspoon per round)
4 ounces (115 grams) butter, softened
1 tablespoon anchovy paste
14 ounces (400 grams) canned artichoke hearts
8 ounces (225 grams) cream cheese, softened
capers for garnish

Cut out bread rounds with a 1½-inch (4-centimeter) cutter. Butter them.

Blend 4 ounces softened butter and the anchovy paste. Spread
thickly on the bread rounds. With a serrated knife, cut well-drained
and dried artichoke hearts crosswise into 2 or 3 slices. Place each
slice on a bread round, pressing it down to secure it. If the slices are
too big to fit on the prepared rounds, cut them into halves or quarters because there must be room to pipe the cream cheese around
them. With a pastry bag or tube, pipe softened cream cheese around
the artichoke slice, anchoring it to the bread and anchovy butter.
Press a caper into the top of each one or a rosette of the cream
cheese. Freeze on a cooky sheet or whatever fits into your freezer
space. When frozen, put the canapés in freezer bags, label, and return to the freezer. *Makes 36 to 40 canapés. Storage time: 2 weeks.*

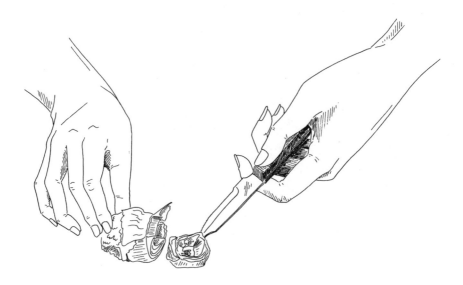

To use: Take the canapés from the freezer bags and arrange on a serving platter. Cover with very damp paper towels. Thaw at room temperature for 1½ to 2 hours. Remove paper towels and serve.

VARIATION:

Omit the cream cheese. Drain and dry the artichoke hearts and slice them into a blender. Melt 4 ounces (115 grams) butter and add it and the anchovy paste to the blender. Blend for a few minutes until mixture becomes puréed. Chill thoroughly. Spread on the prepared bread rounds. Top with a few capers and freeze as directed in the basic recipe. This is a delicious combination of flavors.

ARTICHOKE CUCUMBER DIP

1 cup (¼ liter) minced cucumber (unpeeled if young and tender)
½ teaspoon salt
8 ounces (225 grams) cream cheese
14 ounces (400 grams) canned artichoke hearts, drained, dried, and minced
2 tablespoons anchovy paste
1 tablespoon chopped capers
1 tablespoon minced green pepper
a little sour cream for thinning (to be used after thawing, if needed)
minced parsley, for garnish

Sprinkle the cucumbers with ½ teaspoon salt and mix them around a little with the fingers. Drain them in a colander for 1 hour. Run fresh water over them to rinse off the salt and dry them thoroughly in paper towels, pressing out the water as you do so.

Mash the cheese and add all other ingredients to it except the sour cream and parsley. Mix together well. Pour into a 1-quart (1-liter) freezer container and freeze. *Storage time: 1 month.*

To use: Thaw in the container in the refrigerator for 24 hours. Whip the dip with a wire whisk or fork. Add some of the sour cream, if needed, to give the right consistency for a dip. Pour into a serving bowl, sprinkle with the minced parsley, and surround with interesting crackers or chips.

CUCUMBER MUSHROOM CANAPÉS

1 loaf of oatmeal bread
2½ ounces (75 grams) soft butter for rounds (⅛ teaspoon per
    round)
2 ounces (60 grams) slivered blanched almonds
½ cup (1 deciliter) chopped cucumber (unpeeled if young and
    tender)
  salt
8 ounces (225 grams) cream cheese
4 ounces (115 grams) mushrooms, minced
1½ teaspoons Worcestershire sauce
1 tablespoon chopped chives
1 tablespoon tarragon vinegar
2 tablespoons (30 milliliters) mayonnaise mixed with 1 teaspoon
    ketchup, for garnish

This spread can be frozen in a 1-quart (1-liter) container to be
spread on the rounds another day.

Cut bread rounds with a 1½-inch (4-centimeter) cutter. Butter
them.

Put the almonds on a cooky sheet and into a 400° F. (205° C.)
oven. Watch them carefully and move them around so they do not
get too brown, just a nice golden color. Remove the almonds and
chop them finely.

Put the chopped cucumber in a colander and sprinkle with 1
teaspoon salt. With the fingers, mix salt into cucumbers. Allow cucumbers to drain for 1 hour. Run cold water over them to rinse off
the salt. Dry the cucumbers with paper towels, pressing the water
out as you do so. Mash the cream cheese and add all other ingredients to it, including ½ teaspoon salt, except the mayonnaise mixture. Heap on the prepared rounds. With a pastry bag or tube with
the star fitting, pipe a rosette of the mayonnaise-ketchup mixture on
top. Freeze the canapés on a cooky sheet or whatever fits into your
freezer space. When frozen, put the canapés in freezer bags, label,
and return to the freezer. *Makes about 60 canapés. Storage time: 1
month.*

To use: Remove the canapés from bags and arrange on a serving
platter. Cover with very damp paper towels. Thaw at room temperature for 1½ to 2 hours. Remove paper towels and serve.

To freeze as spread: Freeze the mixture in a 1-quart (1-liter) freezer container.

To use: Thaw in the refrigerator for 24 hours. Turn out on a serving platter and mold the mixture into an interesting shape. Surround with wheat crackers. *Serves 10 to 12 people.*

EGGPLANT CAVIAR

1 pound (450 grams) eggplant
½ teaspoon salt
¼ cup (½ deciliter) olive oil
1 onion, minced
1 small green pepper, minced
1 large garlic clove, put through garlic press
5 tablespoons (½ deciliter) minced stuffed green olives
4 medium-size tomatoes, peeled, seeded and chopped
2 tablespoons (30 milliliters) wine vinegar
2 teaspoons lemon juice
salt and pepper
½ teaspoon minced fresh or dried basil
¼ teaspoon dried thyme

Peel the eggplant and cut into ½-inch (1½-centimeter) cubes. Sprinkle the eggplant cubes with ½ teaspoon salt and put them in a colander for 30 minutes. Rinse with cold water and dry on paper towels. Pour the olive oil into a large skillet and sauté the eggplant, turning it often until it is quite brown. Remove from the pan and set aside. In the same pan, using additional oil if necessary, sauté the onion, green pepper, garlic and 5 tablespoons minced olives until soft and just beginning to brown. Put the eggplant back in the pan and add the tomatoes, vinegar, lemon juice, salt and pepper to taste, basil and thyme. Cook over low heat, stirring often to keep it from sticking, for about 30 minutes. The liquid should be all absorbed and the vegetables mushy. Put in 1-quart (1-liter) freezer containers and freeze. *Serves 10 to 12. Storage time: several months.*

To use: Thaw in the refrigerator for 24 hours. Spoon the eggplant caviar into a pretty serving bowl and surround with crackers or toast cases.

EGGPLANT CANAPÉS

1 loaf of white bread
1½ ounces (45 grams) soft butter for rounds (⅛ teaspoon per
    round)
4 ounces (115 grams) canned eggplant appetizer, or homemade
    Eggplant Caviar (preceding recipe)
1 teaspoon A.1. Sauce or Sauce Robert
1 teaspoon Worcestershire sauce
1 tablespoon chili sauce
1 teaspoon dried dillweed
1½ tablespoons chopped parsley
4 ounces (115 grams) softened cream cheese

Cut out bread rounds with a 1½-inch (4-centimeter) cutter. Butter them.

Chop the eggplant appetizer or eggplant caviar and mix in all
other ingredients except the cream cheese. With a pastry bag or
tube, pipe a border of cream cheese around the edge of the bread
rounds and fill the centers with the eggplant mixture. Freeze the
canapés on a cooky sheet or whatever fits into your freezer space.
When frozen, put the canapés in freezer bags, label, and return to
the freezer. *Makes about 30 canapés. Storage time: 1 month.*

To use: Take the canapés from freezer bags and arrange on a
serving platter. Cover with very damp paper towels. Thaw at room
temperature for 1½ to 2 hours. Remove paper towels and serve.

EGGPLANT WITH PICKLED BEETS

1 loaf of pumpernickel bread
2 ounces (60 grams) soft butter for rounds (⅛ teaspoon per
    round)
4 ounces (115 grams) canned eggplant appetizer, or homemade
    Eggplant Caviar (see Index)
½ cup (1 deciliter) pickled beets
6 ounces (170 grams) cream cheese
2 teaspoons Worcestershire sauce
stuffed green olives, for garnish

Cut out bread rounds with a 1½-inch (4-centimeter) cutter or any shape you wish. Butter them.

Chop the eggplant appetizer. Drain and mince the beets; measure 5 tablespoons for the recipe. Mash the cream cheese in a bowl. Add eggplant, beets and Worcestershire sauce, and mix thoroughly. Spread thickly on the prepared rounds. Top with a slice of olive; press down to secure it. Freeze the canapés on a cooky sheet or whatever fits into your freezer space. When frozen, put the canapés in freezer bags, label, and return to the freezer. *Makes about 45 canapés. Storage time: 1 month.*

To use: Remove the canapés from freezer bags and arrange on a serving platter. Cover with very damp paper towels. Thaw at room temperature for 1½ to 2 hours. Remove paper towels and serve.

EGGPLANT SOUFFLÉ IN TOAST CASES

1 pound (450 grams) eggplant
1 tablespoon butter
1 medium-size onion, minced
1 garlic clove, put through garlic press
1 tablespoon unbleached flour
¾ cup (1½ deciliters) milk
2 tablespoons (30 milliliters) tomato paste
⅛ teaspoon dried thyme
1 ounce (30 grams) Cheddar cheese, grated
¼ teaspoon salt
⅛ teaspoon ground pepper
2 eggs, separated
75 Toast Cases (see Index)

Drop whole eggplant into boiling salted water to cover. Bring to a boil and boil for 25 minutes. Drain and plunge into a bowl of ice water. When cold, slip off the skin and put the pulp in another bowl. Mash the pulp or purée in a blender. Set aside.

Melt the butter and sauté the onion and garlic over low heat until onion is translucent and tender. Add the flour and cook and stir for a few minutes. Slowly add the milk, stirring constantly. When thick and smooth, add the tomato paste, thyme, grated cheese, salt and pepper. When well mixed and cheese is melted, remove from heat and cool, stirring occasionally. When cool, add the 2 egg yolks and the eggplant pulp. Beat thoroughly. Beat the egg whites until stiff. Fold them into the eggplant mixture. Gently spoon into the toast cases. Freeze on a cooky sheet or whatever fits into your freezer space. When frozen, put the eggplant-filled toast cases into freezer bags, label, and return to the freezer. *Makes about 75 souffléed canapés. Storage time: 1 month.*

To use: Place the frozen canapés on a cooky sheet and into a 400° F. (205° C.) oven for 10 minutes, or until heated through and bubbly.

MUSHROOM TURNOVERS

1 tablespoon butter
6 medium-size mushrooms, minced
1 tablespoon minced scallions or onions
1 tablespoon unbleached flour
¼ cup (½ deciliter) heavy cream
½ cup (1 deciliter) beef bouillon
1 ounce (30 milliliters) sherry
1 teaspoon chili sauce
ground pepper
1 tablespoon minced parsley
double recipe of Flaky Pastry (see Index)
1 egg, beaten, for brushing tops of turnovers

Melt butter and add mushrooms and scallions. Cook for 4 minutes. Add flour and cook for a few more minutes. Add cream, bouillon, sherry, chili sauce, and pepper to taste. Cook and stir until thick. Add parsley and cool.

Make Flaky Pastry and roll out ⅛ inch (½ centimeter) thick. Cut into approximately 3-inch (8-centimeter) rounds. Brush the edge of the rounds with the egg. Put about 1 teaspoon of the mushroom mixture on each round. Fold over and seal the edges with the fingers, fork tines or pastry sealer. Brush the tops with the beaten egg. Freeze on a cooky sheet or whatever fits into your freezer space. When frozen, put the turnovers in freezer bags, label, and return to the freezer. *Makes about 40 turnovers. Storage time: 1 to 2 months.*

To use: With a pointed knife, make a very small slit in each frozen turnover. Bake in a 400° F. (205° C.) oven for about 15 minutes, or until lightly browned and heated through.

TURNOVERS

MUSHROOM ANCHOVY CANAPÉS

    1 loaf of whole-wheat bread
    4 ounces (115 grams) canned mushrooms
    1 ounce (30 grams) flat anchovy fillets
    8 ounces (225 grams) cream cheese
    2 tablespoons (30 milliliters) snipped chives
    1 tablespoon chili sauce
    ½ teaspoon dried dillweed
    ground pepper

    Cut rounds out of the bread slices with a 1¾-inch (4½-centimeter) cutter, or cut out rectangles or any other shape you wish. Put them on a cooky sheet and into a 350° F. (180° C.) oven for 5 to 6 minutes. They should bake until they are a little dry to the touch but should not take on any color as they will be baked again later on. Remove the rounds, cover them with a dry towel, and allow to cool.

Drain and chop the mushrooms and anchovies. Mash the cream cheese and add the mushrooms, anchovies, chives and the other ingredients, with pepper to taste. Mix thoroughly. Spread thickly on the prepared toast rounds. Freeze the canapés on a cooky sheet or whatever fits into your freezer space. When frozen, put in freezer bags, label, and return to the freezer. *Makes about 50 canapés. Storage time: 2 weeks.*

To use: Bake in a 350° F. (180° C.) oven for 10 to 15 minutes, or until lightly browned. These could be broiled also; do not set them too close to the source of heat.

STUFFED MUSHROOMS

24 medium-size mushrooms
4 chicken livers
2 ounces (60 grams) butter, melted, or more if needed
1 small onion, minced
1 tablespoon minced parsley
½ teaspoon Worcestershire sauce
1 teaspoon soy sauce
2 teaspoons chili sauce
2 tablespoons (30 milliliters) mayonnaise
Parmesan cheese, grated

Clean the mushrooms with a damp cloth. Remove and chop the stems. Reserve the caps. Parboil the chicken livers in salted water for 3 minutes. Put them through the finest blade of a meat grinder, or blend in blender. Sauté the chopped onion in 1 tablespoon of the butter, until golden and nearly cooked. Add onion to the livers and minced mushroom stems. Add all other ingredients except Parmesan cheese and mushroom caps. Mix together thoroughly. Dip mushroom caps in remaining melted butter and place them dome side down on a cooky sheet or whatever fits into your freezer space. Mound the stuffing mixture on the mushrooms and sprinkle generously with Parmesan cheese. Freeze the stuffed mushrooms. When frozen, put the stuffed mushrooms in freezer bags, label, and return to the freezer. *Makes 24. Storage time: 2 weeks.*

To use: Bake in a 375° F. (190° C.) oven for about 15 minutes, until heated through and golden. Serve with plenty of cocktail napkins.

Mound any leftover mixture in toast cases (see Index). Freeze the same way as the mushrooms.

To use: Bake in the 375° F. (190° C.) oven but for only about 10 minutes.

VARIATION I

> 24 medium-size mushrooms
> ½ cup (1 deciliter) ground cooked ham
> 1 tablespoon minced parsley
> 1 teaspoon minced celery leaves
> 1 teaspoon prepared mustard
> 1 tablespoon dairy sour cream
> 1 tablespoon sherry
> Parmesan cheese
> 2 ounces (60 grams) butter, melted

Prepare the mushrooms as directed in the basic recipe. Mix stuffing ingredients together and stuff the caps. Dribble some melted butter over the Parmesan cheese. Freeze and bake.

VARIATION II:

> 24 medium-size mushrooms
> ½ cup (1 deciliter) minced celery
> 1 teaspoon minced capers
> ½ teaspoon grated onion
> 2 tablespoons (30 milliliters) mayonnaise
> ¼ teaspoon dried tarragon
> ½ teaspoon salt
> ground pepper

Proceed exactly as directed in Variation I.

LOBSTER-STUFFED MUSHROOMS

½ cup (1 deciliter) thick cream sauce
8 ounces (225 grams) small uniform-size mushrooms
1½ ounces (45 grams) butter
8 ounces (225 grams) cooked lobster meat, finely chopped
½ teaspoon curry powder
1 tablespoon chili sauce
1 teaspoon lemon juice
¼ teaspoon grated lemon rind
1 to 1½ ounces (30 to 45 grams) butter, melted

CREAM SAUCE:

1 tablespoon butter
1 tablespoon unbleached flour
¾ cup (1½ deciliters) milk

First make the cream sauce: Melt 1 tablespoon butter in a pan. Add the flour. When well blended, add the milk to make a very thick sauce. Cook, stirring until smooth.

Clean the mushrooms with a damp cloth and remove the stems. Mince the stems. Melt 1½ ounces butter and sauté the minced stems over moderate heat for 4 minutes. Add the lobster, cream sauce, curry powder, chili sauce, lemon juice and rind and mix thoroughly. Dip the mushroom caps in the remaining melted butter and place them, dome side down, on a cooky sheet or whatever fits your freezer space. Stuff the caps with the lobster mixture. There will be some mixture left over. Mound it on some toast rounds. Freeze the stuffed mushrooms and the toast rounds on the cooky sheet. When frozen, put them in freezer bags, label, and return to the freezer. *Makes 15 to 20, depending on the size of the mushroom caps. Storage time: 2 weeks.*

To use: Broil the still frozen mushroom caps for 8 to 10 minutes, until heated through and brown and bubbly. Or bake them in the oven at 400° F. (205° C.) for about 10 minutes, also until brown and bubbly. Do the same with the toast rounds

OYSTER-STUFFED MUSHROOMS

8 ounces (225 grams) fresh mushrooms, as uniformly shaped as possible
1½ ounces (45 grams) butter
1 onion, minced
5 ounces (140 grams) oysters, canned or fresh, drained and minced
1 teaspoon lemon juice
1 tablespoon chili sauce
1 ounce (30 milliliters) sherry
½ teaspoon salt
2 ounces (60 grams) butter, melted, more, if needed

Wipe mushrooms clean with a damp cloth. Remove and mince the stems. Set the caps aside. Melt 1½ ounces butter and sauté the minced onion in it over medium heat, stirring from time to time, for 5 minutes. Add the minced mushroom stems and cook until all the moisture has been drawn out of them, about 5 minutes. Scrape the onion and mushroom-stem mixture into a bowl and add all other ingredients except remaining melted butter and mushroom caps. Mix well. Dip the mushroom caps in melted butter to get them well covered. Place them on a cooky sheet, dome side down. Stuff them with the oyster mixture. There will be some of the mixture left over, so mound it on toast rounds. Freeze the mushrooms and toast rounds on the cooky sheet or whatever fits your freezer space. When frozen, put them in freezer bags, label, and return to the freezer. *Makes 12 to 20 stuffed mushrooms, depending on the size of the mushroom caps, and 12 additional canapés. Storage time: 2 weeks.*

To use: Broil the frozen mushrooms for about 10 minutes, until heated through, brown and bubbly. Or you can bake them in a preheated 400° F. (205° C.) oven for 10 to 15 minutes. These are unusual and delicious. Be sure you have plenty of cocktail napkins when you serve them.

SAUSAGE-STUFFED MUSHROOMS

1 pound (454 grams) little pork sausages, each 4 inches (10 centimeters) long
2 ounces (60 grams) butter
1 medium-size onion, minced
1 small carrot, minced
1 small celery rib, minced
24 mushrooms, 1 to 1½ inches (2½ to 4 centimeters) in diameter
2 tablespoons flour
1 cup (¼ liter) rosé wine
salt

However you buy the sausages, you will need 6 sausages. If you buy them in a package, take out the 6 sausages and put the rest of them in the freezer for another time. Place the sausages in a sauce-pan and cover with cold water. Bring to a boil, then reduce the heat and simmer them for 10 minutes. Remove from water and cool until you can handle them. Meantime, melt 1 ounce of the butter in a fry-ing pan. Add the minced onion, carrot and celery, and sauté gently for 5 minutes. Remove the stems from the mushrooms and set the caps aside. Mince the stems and add them to the frying pan. Sauté for another 5 minutes; do not brown. Take the casing off the sau-sages and mash the meat. Add it to the pan and cook gently for another 5 minutes. Add the flour and cook for a few minutes. When well blended, add the wine. Stir and cook until thick. Add salt to taste.

Melt remaining 1 ounce of butter in a clean pan. Swish the mushroom caps around in it until they are well coated. Place them, dome side down, on a cooky sheet or whatever fits your freezer space, and fill them with the sausage mixture. Freeze the stuffed mushrooms on the cooky sheet. When frozen, put the stuffed mushrooms in freezer bags, label, and return to the freezer. *Makes 24 stuffed mushrooms. Storage time: 2 weeks.*

To use: Place the frozen stuffed mushrooms on a cooky sheet and bake in a 400° F. (205° C.) oven for 12 minutes. Using a slotted spoon, carefully remove them to a serving platter. Serve them to your guests with plenty of cocktail napkins and a warning not to burn themselves, as these are eaten with the fingers.

CURRIED SWEET PICKLED ONION CANAPÉS

1 loaf of white or oatmeal bread
2 ounces (60 grams) soft butter for rounds (⅛ teaspoon per
    round)
8 ounces (225 grams) sweet pickled onions (not sour cocktail
    onions)
8 ounces (225 grams) cream cheese
1 teaspoon Worcestershire sauce
1 tablespoon chopped parsley
1 teaspoon dried dillweed
1 teaspoon curry powder

Cut out bread rounds with a 1½-inch (4-centimeter) cutter or any shape you wish. Butter them.

Reserve 5 onions and mince the rest. Mash the cream cheese and add the minced onions and all other ingredients except reserved 5 onions. Spread on the prepared rounds. With a serrated knife, slice remaining 5 onions. You really can slice these little onions 2 or 3 times across each one. Separate slices into rings and press 1 ring on top of each canapé. Freeze the canapés on a cooky sheet or whatever fits into your freezer space. When frozen, put the canapés in freezer bags, label, and return to the freezer. *Makes 50 to 60 canapés. Storage time: 1 month.*

To use: Remove canapés from the bags and arrange on a serving platter. Cover with very damp paper towels. Thaw at room temperature for 1½ to 2 hours. Remove towels and serve.

GREEN AND RED CANAPÉS

1 loaf of pumpernickel or rye bread
2 ounces (60 grams) soft butter for rounds (⅛ teaspoon per
    round)
2 ounces (60 grams) shelled walnuts
1 green pepper, minced
1 sweet red pepper, minced
8 ounces (225 grams) cream cheese, softened
1 teaspoon Worcestershire sauce
1 tablespoon mayonnaise
2 teaspoons minced parsley
¼ teaspoon dried basil
salt and pepper
slivers of green and red peppers, for garnish

Cut bread rounds with a 1½-inch (4-centimeter) cutter or any
shape you wish. Butter them.

Mince the walnuts. Put all ingredients in a bowl except slivers of
green and red pepper for garnish. Add salt and pepper to taste. Mix
until well blended. Spread generously on the prepared rounds. Top
with slivers of green and red peppers. You might have green on
some and red on others for a pretty effect. Freeze on a cooky sheet
or whatever fits into your freezer space. When frozen, put the canapés in freezer bags, label, and return to the freezer. *Makes about 50
canapés. Storage time: 1 month.*

To use: Remove canapés from the bags and arrange on a serving
platter. Cover with very damp paper towels. Thaw at room temperature for 1½ to 2 hours. Remove paper towels and serve.

PIMIENTO ANCHOVY CANAPÉS

1 loaf of Anadama or oatmeal bread
2 ounces (60 grams) soft butter for the rounds (⅛ teaspoon per
    round)
8 ounces (225 grams) pimientos
8 ounces (225 grams) cream cheese
1 teaspoon anchovy paste, or more to taste
1 tablespoon red-wine vinegar
1 teaspoon dried dillweed
1 teaspoon paprika
½ teaspoon pepper
parsley for garnish

This spread can be frozen in 1-quart (1-liter) freezer containers
to be spread on the rounds another day.

Cut out the bread rounds with a 1½-inch (4-centimeter) cutter.
Butter them.

Drain the pimientos and dry them well. Mince them and mix
with all other ingredients except the parsley for garnish.
Thoroughly blend the mixture and spread thickly on the prepared
rounds. Press a small piece of parsley on the top of each one. Freeze
the canapés on a cooky sheet or whatever fits into your freezer
space. When frozen, put the canapés in freezer bags, label, and return to the freezer. *Makes 50 to 60 canapés. Storage time: 1 month.*

To use: Remove canapés carefully from the bags so as not to
break off the frozen parsley. Place them on a serving platter and
cover with very damp paper towels. Thaw at room temperature for
1½ to 2 hours. Remove paper towels and serve.

To use as a spread: If frozen in freezer containers, just thaw the
spread in the containers in the refrigerator for 24 hours. Put in a
bowl, or mold the pimiento-anchovy mixture into a log or roll. Place
it on a serving platter and surround it with crackers.

PARTY PIZZA

2 tablespoons (30 milliliters) olive oil
1 onion, minced
2 tomatoes, peeled, seeded and chopped
1 garlic clove, minced
6 stuffed green olives, minced
⅛ teaspoon salt
½ teaspoon sugar
½ teaspoon dried orégano
8 ounces (225 grams) mozzarella cheese, shredded
Flaky Pastry (see Index)
2 or 3 flat anchovy fillets
Parmesan cheese

Heat the olive oil in a frying pan and add the onion. Sauté onion until golden and tender. Add the tomatoes, garlic, olives, salt and sugar. Cook gently over low heat until the vegetables are done and the juice from the tomatoes has almost cooked away. Stir occasionally. Add the orégano and remove from the heat. Add 2 tablespoons of the shredded mozzarella cheese to the mixture. Stir until melted. Cool.

Roll out the pastry to a sheet ¼ inch (¾ centimeter) thick, and cut out 2-inch (5-centimeter) rounds with a cooky cutter. I like to shape them like a pea pod. They don't uniformly hold this shape while cooking, but they are pretty and tasty morsels just the same. Put a drop of water on opposite sides of a circle, pinch the edges together at those points, and flatten the bottom to resemble a pea pod. Put ½ teaspoon of the tomato mixture in each one. Top the pastry cases with more mozzarella cheese. Cut an anchovy across in tiny slivers and place a sliver on top. Sprinkle with Parmesan cheese and a drop of olive oil. Freeze the pizzas on a cooky sheet or whatever fits into your freezer space. When frozen, put in freezer bags, label, and return to the freezer. *Makes 20 to 25 party pizzas. Storage time: 1 month.*

To use: Bake in a 400° F. (205° C.) oven for 10 to 12 minutes. The pastry should be light brown and puffy.

Before

After

PARTY PIZZA

SPINACH-FILLED TOAST CASES

1 tablespoon butter
3 tablespoons (45 milliliters) minced onion
2 tablespoons unbleached flour
½ cup (1 deciliter) light cream
14 ounces (675 grams) canned sliced mushrooms
1 cup (¼ liter) cooked spinach, minced (or chard or beet greens)
1 tablespoon sherry
½ teaspoon salt and some ground pepper
24 Toast Cases (see Index)
2 to 3 tablespoons grated Parmesan cheese
2 teaspoons extra butter as topping

Melt the tablespoon of butter and sauté the onion until golden and tender. Add the flour and cook for a few minutes. Slowly add the cream and stir until very thick. Drain the mushrooms, chop them, and add them and the spinach to the cream sauce. Add the sherry, salt and pepper. Fill the toast cases and sprinkle the Parmesan cheese on top. Dot each one with a sliver of butter. Freeze the filled cases on a cooky sheet or whatever fits into your freezer space. When frozen, put the filled cases in freezer bags, being careful not to dislodge the butter on top of the canapés, label, and return to the freezer. *Makes 24 filled cases. Storage time: 1 month.*

To use: Bake the frozen cases in a 400° F. (205° C.) oven for 10 minutes.

SAUCES

COCKTAIL SAUCE

1 cup (¼ liter) mayonnaise
¼ cup (½ deciliter) chili sauce
2 teaspoons prepared mustard
1 teaspoon grated onion
2 tablespoons (30 milliliters) minced gherkins (sweet or dill
     depending on your taste)
1 teaspoon chopped capers
2 teaspoons lemon juice
2 teaspoons dried dill

Put all ingredients in a bowl and whip with a wire whisk. Pour into a 1-pint (½-liter) freezer container, label, and freeze. *Makes 1½ cups (3½ deciliters) and serves about 10 people. Storage time: indefinitely.*

To use: Place the container in the refrigerator 24 hours before needed. Whip sauce with a wire whisk and pour it into a serving bowl. Use as a dip for Bite-Size Fish Balls (see Index).

SAVORY SAUCE

½ cup (1 deciliter) chili sauce
1 cup (¼ liter) dairy sour cream
1 tablespoon chopped capers
1 tablespoon sweet pickle relish, drained
1 teaspoon light brown sugar
1 tablespoon lemon juice
grated rind of ½ lemon
salt

When measuring the relish, put it in a tablespoon and press out the pickle juice with your fingers. Put all ingredients together and mix well with a wire whisk. Add salt to taste. Pour into a 1-pint (½-liter) freezer container, label, and freeze. *Makes 1 pint (½ liter) sauce and serves 15 people. Storage time: indefinitely.*

To use: Thaw in the refrigerator for 24 hours. Use as a dip for Savory Meatballs (see Index). This is delicious with Bite-Size Fish Balls, also, but to use with these omit the brown sugar.

MUSTARD SAUCE

1 ounce (30 grams) butter
2 tablespoons unbleached flour
1 cup (¼ liter) well-seasoned chicken broth
¼ cup (½ deciliter) tarragon vinegar
1 tablespoon dry mustard
1 tablespoon sugar
1 teaspoon lemon juice
1 teaspoon prepared horseradish, drained
salt

Melt butter, add flour, and cook for a few minutes. Add the broth and vinegar and stir over heat until thickened. Mix a little water into the dry mustard and sugar to make a smooth, wet paste. Add this and the lemon juice, horseradish, and salt to taste to the sauce. Mix well. Pour into a freezer container. Put a piece of plastic wrap directly on the surface of the sauce to keep air from reaching it. Cover, cool, and freeze. *Makes 2 cups (½ liter) sauce.*

To use: Place in the refrigerator 24 hours before needed. Put in a metal bowl and cover again, with the plastic wrap directly on the surface of the sauce to keep out the air. This will keep a skin from forming on the surface. At 1 hour before serving time, place the covered bowl over a pan of simmering water. Heat through. Turn off the heat but keep the sauce warm over hot water, stirring occasionally, until serving time.

MUSTARD-CAPER SAUCE

1 cup (¼ liter) mayonnaise
1 tablespoon prepared mustard
1 teaspoon lemon juice
2 teaspoons minced capers
2 teaspoons finely minced parsley

Put all ingredients in a bowl and mix them well. Put the sauce in a freezer container and freeze. *Makes 1½ cups (3½ deciliters) sauce.*

To use: Thaw in the refrigerator for 24 hours. When ready to use, whisk the sauce with a wire whisk and put it in a bowl. Use as a dip for Bite-Size Fish Balls or Ham Potato Balls (see Index for recipes).

RAISIN SAUCE

1 ounce (30 grams) butter
2 tablespoons unbleached flour
10½ ounces (300 grams) consommé, canned or fresh
1 ounce (30 milliliters) sherry
2 tablespoons (30 milliliters) currant jelly
½ cup (1 deciliter) seedless raisins
pinch of dried thyme

Melt butter and add the flour. Cook for a few minutes and slowly add the consommé. Stir until slightly thickened. Add the rest of the ingredients and cook and stir until very smooth. Pour into a freezer container of 1-quart (1-liter) size and cool in the refrigerator. When cold, label the container and freeze. *Makes 2 cups (½ liter) sauce.*

To use: Thaw in the refrigerator overnight. Put in the top part of a double boiler over barely simmering water, and heat the sauce until piping hot. Pour into a serving bowl and serve with ham.

HORSERADISH CREAM
(for cold roast beef)

1 cup (¼ liter) heavy cream
1 tablespoon prepared horseradish, drained, as dry as possible
2 teaspoons prepared Dijon mustard
¼ teaspoon salt

Whip the cream until it is almost but not quite stiff. Add the other ingredients and beat until cream is just stiff enough to hold its shape. With a pastry bag and a large tube with a ½-inch (1½-centimeter) opening, press out on a cooky sheet rosettes 1½ inches (4 centimeters) across and about 1 inch (2½ centimeters) high. Put the rosettes in the freezer and freeze. When frozen, transfer the rosettes to a freezer bag, label, and return to the freezer. If you prefer, you can just use a spoon to put them on the cooky sheet, making a little peak on the top. These whipped cream mounds will not stick together in the bag after they are frozen. *Makes 24 rosettes. Storage time: several weeks.*
NOTE: Make extra Horseradish Cream and freeze it in a labeled container to be served from a bowl with roast beef. Just thaw in the refrigerator for 24 hours. Whip the cream a little with a fork and spoon into a serving bowl.

SWEET-SOUR SAUCE

1 ounce (30 grams) butter
2 medium-size onions, chopped
3 tablespoons flour
2 cups (½ liter) rich chicken broth
3 tablespoons (45 milliliters) wine vinegar
¼ cup (½ deciliter) dark brown sugar
1 tablespoon ketchup
2 teaspoons lemon juice
grated rind of ½ lemon
1 teaspoon prepared mustard
salt

Melt the butter and sauté the onions over medium heat until

cooked and starting to brown. Add the flour and stir for a minute or two. Slowly add the chicken broth, stirring constantly. Add all other ingredients with salt to taste. Cook over low heat, stirring, until thick. Put through a strainer into a bowl. When cool, put the sauce in a 1-quart (1-liter) freezer container and freeze. *Storage time: indefinitely.*

To use: Thaw the sauce in the refrigerator overnight. Put it in the top part of a double boiler and heat over simmering water, stirring occasionally. The sauce will be quite thick; you can thin it, if desired, with a little water or broth.

RÉMOULADE SAUCE

½ cup (1 deciliter) minced sour pickles
1 tablespoon minced parsley
2 tablespoons (30 milliliters) chopped capers
2 cups (½ liter) mayonnaise
1 tablespoon prepared mustard
1 teaspoon mixed dried tarragon and dillweed
1 teaspoon dried chervil
1 tablespoon anchovy paste (optional: good with fish balls)
½ teaspoon lemon juice

Rémoulade sauce is a very old and well-known sauce. Almost every cookbook has a recipe for it and they are all different. For my version, you must look for sour pickles as not all stores carry them. They are better in this sauce than dill pickles. It has been said that mayonnaise can not be frozen without separating. Buy the best mayonnaise you can buy, or make your own in a blender. Never have I experienced any trouble freezing it. Mayonnaise sauces are always whipped again when they are thawed, and they look and taste the way they did before being frozen.

Press the moisture out of the pickles in a paper towel. Mix all ingredients together and put in a 1-pint (½-liter) container and freeze. *Makes 1½ cups (3½ deciliters) sauce.*

To use: Thaw the sauce in the refrigerator for 24 hours before needed. Whip it with a wire whisk and put it in a serving bowl.

COCKTAIL-BUFFET

When is a cocktail party not a cocktail party?

When it's a cocktail-buffet.

In our part of Maine, unless you live "just down the road a piece," you would probably not be asked to drop by for a cocktail the way you do in the city, because the distances are so great between the houses and towns. If you live on one of the peninsulas on the coast and want to visit a friend on another peninsula, you might have to drive thirty or forty miles. Consequently, our cocktail parties consist of fairly substantial hors-d'oeuvre. We want our guests to leave so happy and full of good things to eat that they will have a safe journey home and won't have to prepare dinner when they get there. This means giving our friends a lot more elaborate fare than a few platters of canapés, even though those canapés are very special.

This brings up the question, "when does a cocktail party cease being a cocktail party and become a cocktail-buffet instead?" In our house it is the inclusion of a roast of some kind. The simple "finger food" cocktail-buffet would not require plates or silverware. The slices of beef, turkey or ham would be sliced thin enough to be put on or between slices of very thinly sliced, buttered bread. A whole Brie cheese, a stuffed Edam or Gouda, whole Camemberts or other delightful cheeses would be arranged around the table with lots of triangles of Patty's Melba Toast and buttered bread rounds (using all kinds of breads). Turnovers and pâtés might be in order, as well as stuffed eggs (isn't it too bad that *they* can't be frozen?).

The more elaborate cocktail-buffet would have the same kind of roast, a hot casserole, maybe a salad or soup. It might even include a dessert. As you can see, this type of cocktail-buffet would require plates, forks and maybe spoons; no knives. I have given a few menus as a suggested guide to the more elaborate of these two types of cocktail-buffets. These are not the only ways of planning cocktail-buffets, it's just our way!

The simpler cocktail-buffet would be one where everything is on the table when your guests arrive. If it is a large enough party to use other rooms, you might have bowls of nuts and other kinds of "nibbles" around on the tables. Otherwise, all the food is there to be eaten whenever anyone feels like it.

The more elaborate cocktail-buffet would be different in that there would be a little more to eat away from the main table while sipping your favorite brew. You might have some whole cheese on a cocktail table with appropriate crackers, or perhaps some little cocktail sausages simmering in a chafing dish. Some warm, crisp cheese wafers might be passed. Have bowls of fresh vegetables—cherry tomatoes, carrots, celery and zucchini sticks, with dips—on the buffet table; or have them on the cocktail table to be nibbled during the cocktail festivities. In any event, try not to have too many things to eat *before* your guests are called to the buffet table.

I am a firm believer in doing as much cooking in advance as possible so that my party will be easy for me. There is nothing worse than to start out exhausted when the evening is supposed to be a gay and festive affair. It has happened so many times in the past that I could scarcely remember a conversation the next day, and not because of overindulgence in the liquid refreshment.

Over the years I have gradually added to my list of things that can be frozen successfully. I hope that the following suggestions and menus will help you to have a party of any size and still feel fresh as the proverbial daisy when your guests arrive.

Now, to the setting up of the buffet table: If the space for the party is large and the table of generous size, then all the food, plates, napkins, silverware and coffee could be put on that one table. If the table is small, then the silverware, napkins, coffee and cups could be put on a nearby side table so that they could be picked up on your way to or from serving yourself at the buffet table. The roast, or main dish, should have the place of honor on the table, surrounded by all the other dishes and condiments. My daughter, Jane Breit, has illustrated here a typical cocktail-buffet table. There isn't a set pattern for a cocktail-buffet as there usually is for the buffet dinner party. There can be less order to the presentation of the food. The cocktail-buffet is more informal and more casual.

The purpose of this book is to give you recipes for frozen hors-d'oeuvre and canapés. I will, however, give you the directions for the freezing and thawing of a few other kinds of things.

It is so important to have a roast beef cooked to the rare stage that I have included the recipe for that. There are several other things that are a great addition to the cocktail-buffet that I have included also, even though they are neither hors-d'oeuvre or canapés, but would be more appropriate in a general cookbook.

One of the most successful large cocktail-buffets I have been to recently had thinly sliced rare roast beef as the main dish. My friend and hostess had provided sumptuous pâtés and all manner of other goodies. To everyone's surprise (because it is not seen too often at cocktail-buffets) she had put a large tureen of thick lentil soup on the table. To *her* surprise, it was eagerly and rapidly consumed. The point is that there are no set rules to follow in preparing for one of these parties. Just put a lot of good things to eat in front of a lot of hungry people and it will all disappear. The more things you can take from your freezer, the easier the party will be for you.

The following menus are for the more elaborate cocktail-buffet and can be rearranged to suit your taste. The various canapé spreads in this book can be used to fill turnovers, croustades and bouchées of all kinds. The buffet table might include black and green olives, spiced apples, watermelon pickle and other fancy condiments that accompany well whatever you have chosen as your *pièce de résistance.* Stir your imagination! Get the preparations in the freezer days in advance and relax until the day of the big party. You've got it made!

MENU I

Salmon in Flaky Pastry
Oyster-Stuffed Mushrooms
Shrimp Pâté I or II
Spinach-Filled Toast Cases
Hot Chicken Almond Canapés
Coleslaw
Lots of party rye, party pumpernickel, white bread
    (all buttered) and Patty's Melba Toast
Juniper Hill's Rum and Orange Pound Cake
Coffee

MENU II

Roast Turkey Slices (very thinly sliced)
Onion Sour-Cream Noodle Casserole
Chicken Liver Pâté with Apple, in crock or bowl
Juniper Hill Meat Puffs
Cucumber Mushroom Canapé (spread) in Croûtes
Orange Cranberry Relish
White and Anadama bread slices, buttered
A large bowl of fresh fruit or thawed frozen fruit
Sweet Cookies or Brownies
Coffee

MENU III

Rare Roast Beef (paper-thin slices) with Horseradish Cream
    or Mustard Sauce
Mushroom Turnovers
Ham Potato Balls with Sweet-Sour Sauce in a chafing dish
Chicken Chutney Canapés (spread) in Toast Cases
Salad
Pickled watermelon rind
Cheddar Twists
White or thinly sliced French bread, buttered
Patty's Melba Toast
Lemon Meringue Pie
Coffee

MENU IV

Baked Ham Slices (thinly sliced)
Baked Beans in Red Wine
Batter-Fried Onion Rings
Jane's Party Pâté
Spiced Apples or Applesauce
Lots of different kinds of mustards
Rye and white bread rounds (thinly sliced), buttered
Ice Cream, Cake or Cookies
Coffee

DOWN EAST COLESLAW

This delicious, freezable recipe was given to me by a friend. Living in the "north country," as we do, our vegetable gardens go to bed in October. We always have mountains of beautiful cabbages that can stay only just so long in the barn before the icy thrusts of winter seek them out under their blankets. Bringing them into the cellar is unsatisfactory so we were thrilled when we heard of this fine recipe, tried it, and loved it. This is an ideal dish for the cocktail-buffet table.

> 3½ quarts (3½ liters) shredded cabbage
> 2 green peppers
> 2 onions
> 1 cup (¼ liter) vinegar
> 1 tablespoon salt
> 1 cup (¼ liter) sugar
> 1 cup (¼ liter) salad oil
> ½ teaspoon celery seeds
> ¼ teaspoon ground pepper

Shred the cabbage and green peppers. Chop the onions. Bring the last 6 ingredients to a boil in a saucepan. Put the cabbage, green peppers and onions in a large bowl and pour the boiling vinegar mixture over them. Cover and marinate for 3 hours. Mix and stir 3 to 4 times during that time.

Put the cabbage and the juice, divided evenly, into two 1-quart (1-liter) and 1-pint (½-liter) plastic freezer containers, label, and freeze.

To use: Thaw in the refrigerator for 24 hours. In spite of the freezing process this coleslaw is crisp.

SALMON IN PASTRY

> double recipe Flaky Pastry (see Index)
> 1 tablespoon butter
> 2 tablespoons (30 milliliters) minced onion
> 3 ounces (90 grams) mushrooms, cleaned and minced
> 5 tablespoons (½ deciliter) cooked rice
> 1 celery rib, minced
> ½ teaspoon salt

CREAM SAUCE:

> 1 tablespoon butter
> 2 teaspoons grated onion
> 1½ tablespoons unbleached flour
> ¾ cup (1½ deciliters) milk

SALMON MIXTURE:

> 6½ ounces (195 grams) canned red sockeye salmon, or cooked
>   fresh salmon
> 1 ounce (30 milliliters) sherry
> 4 ounces (115 grams) Cheddar cheese, grated
> grated rind of 1 lemon
> 1 teaspoon lemon juice
> ½ teaspoon dried dillweed
> ground pepper (quite a bit of this)
> 1 egg, slightly beaten
> 1 egg, mixed with 1 teaspoon water

Make the Flaky Pastry and chill it. Roll and chill again. While it is chilling a second time, mix the filling.

Melt 1 tablespoon butter and sauté the *minced* onion and mushrooms until tender. Add the cooked rice, raw celery and salt. Set aside.

Make the sauce: Melt the second tablespoon of butter and sauté the *grated* onion for a few minutes. Add the flour and cook for a few more minutes. Slowly add the milk while stirring. Cook until thick. Add to the mushroom mixture.

Drain the salmon, if canned, and remove the skin and bones. Mash the salmon, add the mushroom and cream-sauce mixture and all the other ingredients except the egg-water mixture. Thoroughly blend these ingredients.

Roll out the pastry ⅛ inch (½ centimeter) thick to a rectangle roughly 22 x 10 inches (55 x 25 centimeters). Cut the edges off to square up the rectangle.

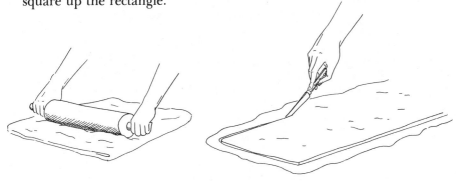

SALMON IN PASTRY

Cut the dough across into halves and slide one half on a cooky sheet. Moisten the edge of it with the egg and water mixture. Spread the salmon mixture on it, keeping it 1 inch (2½ centimeters) in from all the edges. Put the other half of the dough on top of the salmon. Press all the edges together. Turn all the edges up and over on themselves for about ½ inch (1½ centimeters) all the way around to seal in the juices. With the tines of a fork or fingers, seal the edges of the pastry securely. Brush a little of the remaining egg and water mixture all over the top. Freeze. If your freezer space will not accommodate a large cooky sheet then put the pastry on some kind of pan that fits.

When frozen, wrap the pastry in plastic wrap and then in foil. Tape it securely so that no air gets in it. Label and return to the freezer. *Serves 8 to 10 people.*

The scraps of pastry that were trimmed off can be re-rolled and cut into fancy shapes and stuck on top after the pastry is brushed with egg. Brush any design you make with egg, also.

To use: Remove wrapping and place the salmon pastry on a cooky sheet set inside another cooky sheet. Poke 3 or 4 steam holes in the pastry with a sharp knife. Bake in a preheated 425° F. (218° C.) oven for about 20 minutes, or until golden. Check it to see that it doesn't brown too fast. Cover loosely with foil if it does. Turn heat down to 400° F. (205° C.) and bake for another 25 minutes.

This dish is beautiful when the pastry is cut out in the shape of a fish. Use a knife to score the pastry to resemble scales, and make a line for the gills and a dot for the eye.

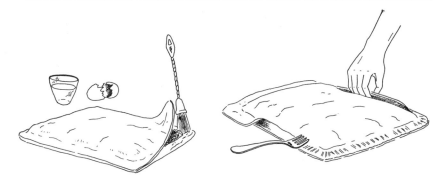

ROAST BEEF SLICES

rolled sirloin tip roast
salt and pepper
vegetable oil
parsley

I am going to give my directions for cooking the beef as it must be rare when served cold. It is also far nicer looking on the buffet table when it's pink instead of gray.

Remove the beef from the refrigerator 1 hour before cooking. Sprinkle with salt, pepper and vegetable oil. Roast in a preheated 300° F. (150° C.) oven for 15 to 18 minutes per pound (per 450 grams). I use the lesser time. Allow ½ pound (225 grams) beef for 4 people. A meat thermometer is useful. Insert it into the center of the beef before cooking. It should register 130° (54° C.) for the rare stage. Remove from oven and cool. Cut into thin slices as your guests will be using forks only. Wrap the slices in plastic wrap, 4 or 5 slices to a package. Press all the air out of the packages. Place in single layers on a cooky sheet or whatever fits into your freezer space. When frozen, put the packages into a large freezer bag, label, and return to the freezer. The advantage of freezing the roast beef slices this way is that you can remove as many or as few as your particular party calls for. *Storage time: 2 weeks.*

To use: Thaw the packages (as many as you will need), unopened and slightly separated, in the refrigerator for 24 hours. On a serving platter, place a slice of beef. Fold it over on itself. Repeat with all of the slices, making neat rows of folded rare beef slices. Tuck some parsley in among the folded beef slices. Serve a rosette of Horseradish Cream on each slice, and have a separate bowl of the cream (see Index) on the table.

TURKEY SLICES

Allow ½ pound (225 grams) turkey per person. This amount is based on the weight of the whole turkey on the market scales. A 14-pound (6½-kilogram) turkey, therefore, would serve 28 people at a party where there were a lot of other added attractions on the buffet table.

Cook the turkey, unstuffed, except for a celery rib, a sliced onion, salt, pepper and dried thyme. Use your favorite recipe but do not overcook the turkey as it would become too dry to freeze successfully. I do mine slowly, with a piece of buttered brown paper on it. It is basted frequently and ends up a nice moist bird.

When just done (or even a little before) remove it from the oven and cover it with foil. When cool, slice it into very thin, even slices. Use only the breast meat and the second joints. Wrap 5 or 6 slices in plastic wrap, pressing out all the air. When you have wrapped them all, put the packages in one layer on a cooky sheet or whatever fits into your freezer space. Freeze. When frozen, put all the packages into one large freezer bag, label, and return to the freezer. *Do not plan to keep the slices longer than 1 to 2 weeks.*

To use: Thaw in the refrigerator, still wrapped, for 24 hours. Separate the individual packages somewhat so they will thaw uniformly. Just before your party, put the slices on a serving platter, decorate with pretty greens, and cover with plastic wrap. At serving time, remove wrap and place turkey on the buffet table.

ORANGE CRANBERRY RELISH

2 large oranges
1 pound (450 grams) cranberries
2 ounces (60 grams) shelled walnuts (optional)
2 cups (285 grams) sugar

Cut the oranges into halves and remove all the seeds. Put the cranberries, unpeeled oranges, and walnuts if used, through the finest blade of a meat grinder. Add sugar and mix it in well. Put in glass jars. This can be frozen but it need not be, as it keeps in the refrigerator for weeks and weeks. If you wish to freeze it, put it in freezer containers, label, and freeze. *It keeps in the freezer for at least a year. Makes 2 quarts (2 liters).*

BAKED HAM SLICES

Cook a ham according to your favorite recipe and cool it thoroughly. Cut the ham into very thin, even slices. Remember that you will not have knives on the table, so cut thin slices. Put 5 or 6 slices in a piece of foil and press all the air out of the package. Proceed in this manner until you have wrapped up all the slices you are going to freeze. Freeze on a cooky sheet or whatever fits best in your freezer space. Keep them in one layer, if possible, so they will freeze quickly. When frozen, put all the packages in one large freezer bag, label, and return to the freezer. *Storage time: 1 month.*

To use hot: Thaw in the foil in the refrigerator overnight. About 30 minutes before you plan to serve the ham, put the packages, still wrapped in foil, in a 350° F. (180° C.) oven. Bake for 20 to 30 minutes, just to heat them through. Unwrap and serve with Raisin Sauce (see Index).

To serve cold: Follow the same thawing directions. Put the ham slices on a serving platter and serve surrounded by delectable condiments, such as spiced apple rings, fancy mustard or spicy applesauce (a bit of horseradish added to it).

ONION SOUR-CREAM NOODLE CASSEROLE

12 ounces (340 grams) medium noodles
1½ cups (3½ deciliters) cottage cheese
1½ cups (3½ deciliters) dairy sour cream
1½ ounces (45 grams) butter
½ cup (1 deciliter) minced onion
1 garlic clove, minced
1½ pounds (675 grams) ground beef
10¾ ounces (305 grams) canned tomato soup
1 teaspoon salt
1 tablespoon Worcestershire sauce
ground pepper
2 tablespoons minced parsley
1½ ounces (45 milliliters) sherry
4 ounces (115 grams) Cheddar cheese, grated

Cook the noodles according to package directions. Drain. Add the cottage cheese and sour cream to them and mix well. Put in 1-quart (1-liter) freezer containers and freeze.

Melt the butter and add the onion and garlic. Cook gently until onion is translucent and tender. Push to one side and add the beef. Cook until it is no longer pink. Add the tomato soup, salt, Worcestershire sauce, pepper and parsley. Stir to mix, then cover and simmer for about 10 minutes. Cool and add the sherry. Put the meat mixture in two 1-quart (1-liter) freezer containers and freeze.

To use: Thaw the containers in the refrigerator for 24 hours. Whisk both mixtures with a fork. Put half of the noodle mixture in the bottom of a buttered 3-quart (3-liter) casserole. Spread half the meat mixture on it. Add one more layer of noodles, then another layer of meat. Sprinkle with the grated Cheddar cheese and bake in a 350° F. (180° C.) oven for 40 minutes.

If you prefer, assemble the ingredients in a freezerproof and ovenproof serving casserole and freeze. Label.

To use: Thaw in the refrigerator for 24 hours and bake as directed.

BATTER-FRIED ONION RINGS

1 egg
¾ cup (1½ deciliters) warm water
1 tablespoon vegetable oil
1 cup (140 grams) flour
¾ teaspoon salt
1 teaspoon sugar
4 large Bermuda onions
½ cup (70 grams) flour, to coat slices
vegetable oil for deep-frying

Beat the egg and add the warm water and oil. Add 1 cup flour, the salt and sugar, and beat until smooth. Cover and refrigerate for 1 hour.

Cut the onions into ¼-inch (¾-centimeter) slices and separate them into rings. Put the extra flour in a paper bag and add the onions to it. Shake them around until they are coated.

When the hour is up, heat the oil to 370° F. (188° C.). With a fork, dip onion rings into the batter, letting excess batter drip off them before putting them in the hot oil. Do only 6 or 7 rings at a time. Fry them until they are golden, about 3 minutes. Remove them with a slotted spoon and drain on absorbent paper. Immediately sprinkle with some salt. Cool thoroughly. Put in 1-quart (1-liter) bags and freeze. You can get about 30 medium-size rings in a bag. *Serves 20 people. Storage time: 1 month.*

To use: Put the onion rings, still frozen, on a baking sheet. Put them in a preheated 400° F. (205° C.) oven for 5 minutes, just to heat through and crisp up again. Put an ovenproof serving bowl in the oven at the same time. Serve the onion rings in it so they will stay hot.

BAKED BEANS IN RED WINE

3 ounces (90 grams) butter
6 or 7 medium-size onions, chopped
1 garlic clove, minced
6 ounces (180 grams) tomato paste
2 tablespoons (30 milliliters) molasses
⅛ teaspoon dried thyme
2 teaspoons prepared mustard
1 cup (¼ liter) dry red wine
4 pounds (1.8 kilograms) canned baked pea beans
4 ounces (1 deciliter) sherry

Melt butter and sauté the onions until they are golden and tender. Put them in a bowl with all the other ingredients except the sherry. Mix carefully so that you do not mash the beans. Put the beans in a freezerproof casserole. Bake in a 350° F. (180° C.) oven, uncovered, for 45 minutes. Cool completely. Cover tightly with foil and tape it on securely. Freeze. *Serves 8 to 10 people. Storage time: 1 month.*

To use: Thaw in the refrigerator overnight. Put in a 350° F. (180° C.) oven. Bake for 20 minutes. Add the sherry, stir gently, and cook for an additional 30 minutes. Serve hot and bubbly.

JUNIPER HILL'S RUM AND ORANGE POUND CAKE

5½ ounces (150 grams) butter, softened
1¼ cups (175 grams) sugar
½ cup (1 deciliter) orange juice
grated rind of 2 oranges
2 ounces (½ deciliter) dark rum
2½ cups (355 grams) sifted cake flour
1¼ teaspoons salt
1 teaspoon baking powder
3 eggs
2¾ ounces (78 grams) slivered almonds, ground or pulverized
    in a blender
½ teaspoon lemon extract

Cream butter and sugar together until fluffy and almost white in color. Add orange juice, grated rind and rum and mix just a little. Sift flour, salt and baking powder and stir into the butter mixture. Beat for several minutes. Add eggs one at a time and beat for 1 minute after each addition. Add ground almonds and lemon extract. Beat for 1 minute and pour into a well-buttered loaf pan measuring 9 x 5 x 2½ inches (23 x 13 x 6½ centimeters). Bake in a 300° F. (145° C.) oven for 1½ hours. Cool in the pan for 10 minutes, then turn out on a cake rack. Cool. Place in a large freezer bag and freeze. *Makes about 35 thin slices.*

To use: Thaw the cake, still in its bag, at room temperature for 24 hours. Slice very thin and make tiny sandwiches with whipped unsalted butter, or softened whipped cream cheese. These are delicious with Champagne, punch, eggnog, coffee or tea.

LEMON MERINGUE PIE

One does not see this kind of pie at a fancy party anymore. It seems to be considered old-fashioned, ordinary, too common, or some such thing. This recipe produces one of the most delightful, prettiest-to-look-at, and heavenly-to-eat desserts a guest could have at a cocktail-buffet party. The fact that it is not made too much for epicurean parties anymore makes it a surprising novelty. Try it and see if you don't get the raves this particular pastry deserves.

PASTRY:

> 1 cup (140 grams) unbleached flour
> 1 tablespoon sugar
> ¼ teaspoon salt
> 1 teaspoon baking powder
> 1 teaspoon grated lemon rind
> 4 ounces (115 grams) butter
> 1½ tablespoons cold water

Sift the flour, sugar, salt and baking powder into a bowl. Add the lemon rind. Slice the butter into the bowl; with a pastry blender or the tips of the fingers, work the butter into the flour. Keep working it until the mixture looks like oatmeal flakes. Now add the water and very quickly mix it in with a fork or the fingertips until dough holds together. Form into a flattened ball, wrap in plastic wrap, and chill for 30 minutes.

Flour a board and put the ball of dough on it. Flour the rolling pin and roll the dough out about 1 inch (2½ centimeters) larger than the pie plate. Set dough in the pie plate and trim off the ragged edge. Make a decorative edge with the fingertips. Prick the bottom and sides all over with the tines of a fork. Bake in a 400° F. (205° C.) oven for about 12 minutes. Remove and cool. Don't worry if the piecrust bubbles up from the bottom of the pie plate.

FILLING:

> 3 eggs, separated
> ⅔ cup (100 grams) sugar
> ¼ cup (½ deciliter) lemon juice
> 1¼ cups (3 deciliters) water
> grated rind of 1 lemon
> 1 tablespoon butter
> ⅛ teaspoon salt
> 3½ tablespoons cornstarch

Put the egg yolks in the top part of a nonaluminum double boiler and mix them around to break them up. Add all the other ingredients except the egg whites, and mix thoroughly. Cook over simmering water until the mixture is thick and creamy. Remove from heat and cool.

Spoon the cooled filling into the pastry shell, and freeze the pie. When frozen, put it very carefully in a large freezer bag, label, and put it in a spot in your freezer where it won't get banged about and the crust broken. Freeze the 3 egg whites in a separate container, labeled. *One pie serves 6 to 8 people. Storage time: 1 month.*

MERINGUE:

> 3 egg whites
> 3 tablespoons sugar
> ¼ teaspoon cream of tartar

Thaw the pie and egg whites, unopened, in the refrigerator for 24 hours. A few hours before your party, beat the egg whites until stiff. Add the sugar, a spoonful at a time, while continuing to beat. Add the cream of tartar and beat until the meringue holds soft peaks. Spread over the lemon filling; make sure meringue is touching the edge of the piecrust all around. Swirl it into pretty peaks. Bake in a 450° F. (230° C.) oven for 2 to 3 minutes, just until the meringue takes on a little color.

RECEPTIONS

(Champagne, Punch, Eggnog, Tea or Coffee Parties)

It will be embarrassing to expose the fact that I've not always been the efficient, well-organized, unflappable person that I have tried to convince myself (and the world) that I am. However, perhaps to prevent the kind of catastrophe happening to you that did happen to me, I will tell all and expect the laughter to echo all the way to Maine.

When my first daughter was married, the wedding was at home. The big freezer on the open back porch was packed with festive fare, since I had had many weeks to prepare the hors-d'oeuvre and had spent countless happy hours doing so. We served Champagne so the hors-d'oeuvre were of a different variety from those one might have with, say, a Martini or a Manhattan.

The wedding cake was a big challenge to me. I had never done one before and it took me several days to make. A lot of loving care was taken with the baking and decorating of this cake. As it was lowered into place at the bottom of my freezer, I thought it looked quite professional with its little yellow flowers and tiny blue forget-me-nots cascading down over the sides.

The delightful rehearsal dinner, which was held the night before the wedding, sent my family and me home in great spirits (in every sense of the word). The removal of the cake from the freezer was our last order of business for the day, so we did just that and brought it in to the kitchen to thaw overnight. To us, it looked magnificent and very, very beautiful sitting there on the counter. We admired it a few moments more before retiring.

The next day, only two hours before we were to leave for the church, I went out to my freezer to remove the hors-d'oeuvre—six hundred of them. I blanch even now when I remember the sight that greeted me on that beautiful, hot August afternoon. Two baskets full of hors-d'oeuvre were on the floor of the porch in the hot sun and the temperature was 85° F. in the shade!

We had been so involved the night before with the successful maneuvering of my precious work of art from freezer to kitchen, that we had completely neglected to return the baskets to their frozen environment. Lest our guests remember our daughter's wedding day by having an acute attack of food poisoning, I was forced to give three hundred hors-d'oeuvre the heave-ho! What a horrible decision to have to make!

Fortunately, my wonderful kitchen helper saved the day by making one hundred and fifty canapés and tiny sandwiches while we were at the church. Added to the three hundred that I still had in the freezer, we didn't fare too badly, but I could have wept when I remembered the caviar, shrimp with mushrooms and other assorted goodies which could never be sampled by our wedding guests.

The moral of this sad tale is that if *you* are solely in charge of food preparation for a wedding, keep your head, heart and mind clear and effective. Don't relax until you see those two happy young people setting off into the sunset with the rice flying and the tin cans banging behind their car!

The art of "designing" a beautiful table of hors-d'oeuvre is one that can be acquired easily, but it helps if you were lucky enough to have been born an aware and observant person.

Study buffet tables in home magazines, cooking magazines, cookbooks or wherever pictures of party tables might appear. At cocktail parties and buffets, notice the way your friends have arranged the food; what is great about it and what might not be so great. The arrangement of the various platters and the flow of traffic are important things to think about, so make mental notes to refer to when planning future parties of your own.

I usually choose the tablecloth first. Since I have a large flower garden, I generally select a cloth that will complement whatever flower is blooming most prolifically at the time. I quite often use the colorful spreads that are made in India; I have quite a collection of them. They brighten up a cold winter day and look equally well with the posies of summer.

You will not need knives or forks on the table but you should have little containers of cocktail picks (colored or plain), and plenty of cocktail napkins. If you own any tiny cocktail forks, you might put them beside a crock of olives, pickled herring or pickles, as you know how hard they are to get out of any container! When I use the Indian spreads, I use stoneware crocks and containers for pâtés and spreads. Wooden trays and baskets are suitable for breads, turnovers and other pastries. It is best to use very plain platters to hold the other hors-d'oeuvre as the cloth and flowers make things look lively and you do want to be able to see the pretty canapés that you've prepared for your guests' delight.

If you use a solid color cloth, or no cloth at all, you could use your fanciest china and silver platters. Pick the flowers, or buy them, to complement your china, or select fruit for a centerpiece with a mental picture of the colors in the platters you plan to use. Make the table a pretty one; it makes everything look and taste better.

A free-standing table is ideal for the larger party, better than a table up against a wall. It makes for a better flow of traffic around the room. If you have several rooms at your disposal, you might have platters of hors-d'oeuvre in each one. If you are serving punch or eggnog, you might have extra punch bowls in other rooms as well. If you are fortunate enough to have hired help (or other family members), the canapés could be passed around from time to time, which generally eliminates the solid lump of people around the main punch and canapé table.

The main thing is to get those hors-d'oeuvre made weeks in advance so that you, too, can enjoy your party to the hilt.

Champagne Party

What you serve at a party where Champagne is the principle liquid refreshment depends a lot on the hour of your party. If it is a noon or evening wedding, for instance, you would choose a menu from the chapter, "Cocktail-Buffet," as it would be more a lunch or dinner kind of menu. If it is an afternoon wedding, as many of them are, you might use a combination of cocktail hors-d'oeuvre and sandwiches. You would have a cake and, of course, coffee.

It might be interesting and informative for the party giver to have some idea of how much Champagne to order. It is a dreadful situation to have a lot of thirsty, expectant guests looking around for more Champagne when it has just run out. It is far better to have too much. You can always use it up eventually, or you might even be able to return it to the store, if you have made that arrangement in advance. When I look at the figures for one of my daughters' weddings, I can't believe that so much Champagne was used. It was not a long or wild reception either, but the wine did disappear.

If Champagne is the only liquid refreshment at the party, you might like to know a few statistics: There are 8 to 10 glasses of Champagne in a bottle. Therefore, as an example, if one's guests were to average 2 glasses of wine apiece, one would need 5 bottles of it for 20 people. If they were thirstier than that and averaged 3 glasses apiece, it would take 6 to 7 bottles to quench their thirst. If the figures for the wedding reception for my daughter are to be believed, our guests averaged 4 plus glasses each. I do seem to remember that there were a few bottles left over so maybe it wasn't the bash that it looks on paper.

There are many other happy occasions when Champagne is served: birthday milestones, baby showers, promotions, successful opening nights, or maybe just a reunion of old friends. Whatever the occasion, I feel certain that you will find some things to make in advance from the list of hors-d'oeuvre in the suggested menus that follow.

AFTERNOON OR LATE NIGHT PARTY
(after the theater, perhaps)
MENU V

Cheese Chutney Ribbon Sandwiches
Chicken Almond Canapés (cold or hot)
Cheese Almond Crispies
Shrimp Mushroom Canapés
Spinach in Toast Cases
Blue-Cheese Caviar Canapés
Cake, Cookies and Coffee

MENU VI

Chicken Pinwheels
Cucumber Coconut Sandwiches
Ham Pinwheels
Eggplant Canapés
Liver Canapés I
Ham Canapés with Walnuts
Hot Oyster Bacon Canapés
Juniper Hill's Rum and Orange Pound Cake
Coffee

MENU VII

Spicy Crab-Meat Patties
Cheddar Twists
Dried Beef Roll
Fancy Seafood Ribbon Sandwich
Chicken Chutney Canapés
Chicken Artichoke Canapés
Cucumber Mushroom Canapés
Cake, Cookies and Coffee

Eggnog Party

The very words "eggnog party" bring to my mind nostalgic, pine-scented, woodsmoke-filled thoughts—holly berries, plum pudding, family, friends, laughter and song. When else but Christmas and New Year's week do people drink the lovely eggnog? I can't remember hearing about anyone sipping that delectable concoction while watching skyrockets, Roman candles and sparklers of a Fourth of July evening. It doesn't go with heat and mosquitoes. It goes best with all the exciting things that happen at the end of one year and the beginning of the next.

One of my favorite parties to give, and to go to, is a New Year's Day eggnog party at 12 o'clock noon. If I stayed up late to watch the New Year in and was a little slow to rise, a cup of hot coffee and toast would be sufficient to see me through until the magical noon hour.

If the eggnog party is being given at my house, the table will have been set the night before. Generally, I write cards and put them on the table to indicate the places where I wish to put the various platters of hors-d'oeuvre, to show them off to the best advantage. This is not a job successfully done on New Year's morning.

Pâtés would have been removed from the freezer and refrigerated at noon the day before. Other kinds of hors-d'oeuvre would come out of the freezer at about 10 o'clock in the morning the day of the party. Arranging and decorating them on the platters might accompany my morning coffee and toast. I would then put the platters on the table where indicated, still covered with their damp paper towels, as described in "To Thaw Bread Canapés." Just before my guests arrive, I would put the bowl of eggnog on the table in its appointed place and remove the towels from all the hors-d'oeuvre. Because of the cards on the table, I am reminded that there is a pâté to be removed from the refrigerator. After a few guests have arrived, the hot hors-d'oeuvre would be popped into the preheated oven.

As for the eggnog, I'll give you my favorite recipe, which was given to me by a friend years ago. It is smooth as silk but not as rich as some of the recipes you might come across in other cookbooks.

EGGNOG

12 eggs, separated	1 quart (1 liter) bourbon
1½ cups (215 grams) sugar	(my favorite), rum or
1 quart (1 liter) whipping cream	brandy
2 quarts (2 liters) milk	nutmeg

Beat the egg yolks until thick. Add the sugar and continue to beat until light and creamy. Whip the cream and alternately stir it and the milk into the egg mixture. Gradually pour in the liquor, stirring constantly. Cover with plastic wrap and refrigerate for at least 24 hours to mellow. Put the egg whites in a separate container and refrigerate, also. About 30 minutes before the first guest is expected, pour the eggnog into a large serving bowl. Whip the egg whites until stiff but not dry. Fold them into the eggnog, and sprinkle the top with a little nutmeg. (If you wish, you can add the beaten egg whites to the eggnog 24 hours ahead.) Put on your best "Happy New Year" smile to greet your guests. If you have taste-tested the gorgeous brew to be sure it is just right, the smile comes easily.

Fortunately for the calorie counters, this day should bring an end to the holiday festivities. I doubt that anyone will be counting calories until January 2nd.

Having thrown out the calorie chart, select some of the hors-d'oeuvre and canapés from the following list of suggestions.

HORS-D'OEUVRE FOR THE EGGNOG PARTY
MENU VIII

Cheese Almond Crispies

Bite-Size Fish Balls

Cold Crab-Meat Canapés

Shrimp Mushroom Canapés

Cheese Chutney Ribbon Sandwiches

Dried Beef Rolls

Juniper Hill's Rum and Orange Pound Cake

Red Caviar Celery Canapés

Curried Camembert Canapés

Stuffed Edam with Pickled Onions

Use 5 to 6 of these recipes at one party. They all go well together. (See Index for pages.)

Punch Party

The purpose of this book is to encourage the reader to make and freeze all manner of goodies for the day of a big party. So far, I have not come across a good punch that benefits from such treatment so I'll not go into the recipes for punches, except one—Strawberry Punch. This is a lovely punch on a hot summer day, or any day for that matter. It is *not* a frozen punch.

The setup of the table would be similar to that for any reception. If it is a large enough party to use more than one room, you should have an additional punch bowl in another room, with canapés. Keep the punch cold, whatever kind it is, and the bowl reasonably full at all times.

Following the Strawberry Punch recipe are two sample lists of hors-d'oeuvre you might use for the punch party. The choices are interchangeable with those given for Champagne, so you might like to look that list over as well.

STRAWBERRY PUNCH

STEP ONE, THE INFUSION:

> 1 quart (450 grams) fresh strawberries, or 1 pound (454 grams) frozen strawberries
> 2 cups (½ liter) dry white wine
> ½ cup (100 grams) sugar
> 1 cup (¼ liter) water

STEP TWO, THE MIXING:

> 3 cups (¾ liter) dry white wine, chilled
> 1 quart (1 liter) Champagne, chilled (if you don't feel rich, 1 quart (1 liter) club soda, chilled)
> 1 large block of ice (freeze this in a bowl and turn it out)
> 1 or 2 sprigs of fresh mint

Put fresh or partially thawed berries in a bowl, squash them a little, and add 2 cups (½ liter) wine. Cover and marinate at room temperature for 2 hours. In the case of the frozen berries, it takes several hours longer to have them completely thawed.

Put the sugar and water in a saucepan. Bring to a boil and simmer for 5 minutes. Put the berries and the marinating wine in a blender and blend on high speed for 1 minute. You may have to do this in 2 batches. Slowly pour in the hot syrup and blend for another minute. Strain through a fine strainer. This procedure should remove all the tiny strawberry seeds. Chill the infusion, covered, in the refrigerator.

When ready to serve, place the block of ice in a large punch bowl. Pour the strawberry infusion over it, then the wine and Champagne or soda. Stir gently as you pour and get the mixture well blended. Wash the mint leaves and float them on top.

Makes 3 quarts (3 liters) of punch and fills 25 punch cups, more as the ice melts.

NOTE: Fresh strawberries are preferred to the frozen ones, but sometimes in the winter you might like to make this punch and the frozen ones are an acceptable substitute.

MENU IX

Stuffed Mushrooms with chicken livers
Ham Chicken Rolls
Salmon Pinwheels
Caviar Canapés
Cucumber Sandwiches

MENU X

Hot Liver Pâté Canapés with Orange
Curried Sweet Pickled Onion Canapés
Cheese Puffs with Blue Cheese Cream
Mushroom Turnovers
Cheese Chutney Ribbon Sandwiches

These menus are interchangeable
as the recipes given all go
equally well with each other.

Tea or Coffee Party

This might be a wedding or a baby shower, or perhaps you might be gathering a few people together to meet the aspiring "Senator-to-be." Whatever the occasion, you will be well prepared if you've got a stock of hors-d'oeuvre stashed in the freezer.

Small sandwiches and turnovers of all kinds are appropriate, as are cake and cookies. Your favorite brownie recipe would go well, also, with tea and coffee. Following the Tea and Coffee recipes are a few suggestions for hors-d'oeuvre.

TEA FOR A CROWD

To make tea for a large crowd, use an earthenware, china or glass container and fill it with boiling water. When the container is hot, pour out the water and put loose tea in it: 1 teaspoon tea and ½ cup (1 deciliter) boiling water per cup. Allow to steep, covered, for 4 to 5 minutes. Strain and throw out the used tea leaves. Keep the infusion warm.

To serve: Put fresh boiling water into the tea infusion to the strength and taste you like.

COFFEE FOR A CROWD
(40 to 50 people)

Use a glass, enamelware or earthenware container. Put 1 pound (450 grams) medium-grind coffee in about 6 layers of cheesecloth large enough to hold it. Allow for the expansion of the coffee grounds. Tie a string around the top. Bring 6 to 8 quarts (6 to 8 liters) water to a rapid boil. Drop in the coffee bag. Turn off the heat and allow the coffee to stand, covered, in a warm place for about 10 minutes, agitating it several times. Remove the bag and keep the coffee hot.

MENU XI

Fancy Seafood Ribbon Sandwich
Brie Cheese with Toasted Almonds
Hot Crab-Meat Turnovers
Chicken Roll (Variation of Dried Beef Roll)
Cheese Wafers
Juniper Hill's Rum and Orange Pound Cake

MENU XII

Ham Chutney Rolls
Eggplant Canapés
Artichoke Canapés
Chicken Pinwheels
Pastry Puffs, filled with Lobster Mushroom Canapé mixture
Juniper Hill's Rum and Orange Pound Cake (this keeps turning up because it is so good with all these things)

CHEESE CHUTNEY RIBBON SANDWICHES

1 loaf of white bread, unsliced
1 loaf of Anadama or oatmeal bread, unsliced
3 ounces (90 grams) shredded coconut
2 tablespoons (30 milliliters) chopped chutney
8 ounces (225 grams) cream cheese
1½ ounces (45 grams) butter, softened
1 teaspoon curry powder
2 tablespoons (30 milliliters) mayonnaise
⅛ teaspoon salt
8 ounces (225 grams) soft butter for buttering the slices

You should always use a white bread and a darker bread for contrast. Slice the bread very thin, no more than ¼ inch (¾ centimeter) thick. Stack slices together, 5 or 6 deep, and trim off the crusts. Slices should then be 4¼ × 3¾ inches (10¾ × 10 centimeters) in size.

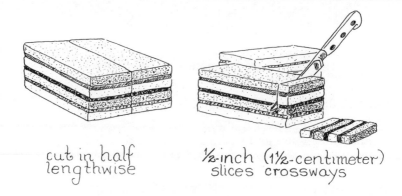

cut in half
lengthwise

½-inch (1½-centimeter)
slices crossways

Put the coconut on a cooky sheet and under a broiler. Toast it until it is a deep golden brown, for 3 to 4 minutes. Move it around a little while it is browning but under no circumstances let it burn.

Mince chutney. Mash the cheese with a fork. Put all ingredients together in a bowl, including the coconut, but not the 8 ounces butter for the slices; mix thoroughly. Spread a slice of bread with 1 teaspoon of the soft butter. Spread it with 1 tablespoon of the chutney mixture. Cover with another slice and repeat. Put 5 or 6 slices together in this fashion and press them firmly together. With a sharp knife, slice down through all the layers, cutting the whole stack of slices into halves. Cut each half into ½-inch (1½-centimeter) slices, putting them on a cooky sheet as you do so. From store loaves you would get about 18 ribbon sandwiches per stack and from Juniper Hill Bread you get about 24 sandwiches per stack.

Freeze the sandwiches on a cooky sheet or whatever fits your freezer space. When frozen, put the sandwiches in freezer bags, label, and return to the freezer. *Storage time: 1 month, or more.*

To use: Place frozen sandwiches on a serving platter and cover with very damp paper towels. Thaw at room temperature for 1½ to 2 hours. Remove paper towels and serve.
NOTE: 2 loaves of Juniper Hill Bread (see Index) will make slightly more than 100 ribbon sandwiches.

CUCUMBER COCONUT CANAPÉS OR SANDWICHES

1 loaf of white bread
2 ounces (60 grams) soft butter for rounds (⅛ teaspoon per round)
1 cup (¼ liter) minced cucumber
½ teaspoon salt
¼ cup (½ deciliter) shredded coconut
2¾ ounces (78 grams) slivered blanched almonds
4 ounces (115 grams) cream cheese
3 tablespoons (45 milliliters) mayonnaise

Cut out the bread rounds with a 1½-inch (4-centimeter) cutter or make them any shape you wish. Butter them.

Place cucumber in a strainer (preferably enamel) and sprinkle with ½ teaspoon salt. Mix cucumber around so that the salt gets on all of it. Allow to sit for 1 hour. Rinse under cold water and drain. Pat dry, pressing the water out of the cucumber.

Put the coconut on a cooky sheet and into a 400° F. (205° C.) oven. Watch it very carefully and stir it around so that it becomes an even golden brown. Remove from the oven and from the cooky sheet and cool for 5 minutes.

If you think you can watch two things in the oven at the same time, stirring both, then put the almonds in at the same time as the coconut. They both get browned in the same temperature, although the almonds take a little longer than the coconut. However you do it, brown them both to a golden color.

Pulverize the toasted almonds in a blender or food processor. Mash the cheese and add remaining ingredients except the mayonnaise. Mix well and spread on the prepared rounds. Decorate the canapés with a rosette of mayonnaise put through a pastry bag or tube. These may be served as open sandwiches, or another round of buttered bread may be placed on top. Freeze the canapés on a cooky sheet or whatever fits into your freezer space. When frozen, put the canapés in freezer bags, label, and return to the freezer. *Makes 30 to 35 canapés or sandwiches. Storage time: 1 month.*

To use: Put frozen canapés on a serving platter and cover with very damp paper towels. Thaw at room temperature for 1½ to 2 hours. Remove paper towels and serve. These are especially good with Champagne.

DATE ORANGE CANAPÉS

2¾ ounces (78 grams) slivered blanched almonds
1 loaf of Anadama bread
3 ounces (90 grams) butter for the rounds (⅛ teaspoon per round)
8 ounces (225 grams) cream cheese
1 ounce (30 grams) butter
4 ounces (115 grams) pitted dates
1 teaspoon grated orange rind
2 tablespoons (30 milliliters) orange juice
1 tablespoon minced chutney

Put the almonds on a cooky sheet and into a 400° F. (205° C.) oven for a few minutes. Watch them carefully so they do not burn. Bake until they are a nice golden color. Remove and cool.

Cut out the bread rounds with a 1½-inch (4-centimeter) cutter. Butter them.

Mash the cheese and remaining 1 ounce of butter together. Put the dates through the finest blade of a meat grinder. Add them, the orange rind and juice and the chutney to the cheese; mix thoroughly. Spread on the prepared rounds. Put 1 or 2 toasted slivered almonds on the top of each round. Place on a cooky sheet or whatever fits into your freezer space. When frozen, put the canapés in freezer bags, label, and return to the freezer. *Makes 50 to 60 canapés. Storage time: several months.*

To use: Place frozen hors-d'oeuvre on a serving platter and cover with very damp paper towels. Thaw at room temperature for 1½ to 2 hours. Remove paper towels and serve.
NOTE: These are especially good with Champagne and other wines and with eggnog.

DATE WALNUT CANAPÉS

1 loaf of Anadama bread
3 ounces (90 grams) butter for rounds (⅛ teaspoon per round)
8 ounces (225 grams) cream cheese
1 ounce (30 grams) butter
8 ounces (225 grams) pitted dates
2 ounces (60 grams) shelled walnuts
½ teaspoon salt
1 tablespoon Worcestershire sauce
2 tablespoons (30 milliliters) mayonnaise for garnish

Cut 1½-inch (4-centimeter) rounds of bread. Butter them.

Mash the cheese and the remaining 1 ounce of butter together. Put the dates and the nuts through the finest blade of a meat grinder. Add them, the salt and Worcestershire sauce, and mix well. Spread on the rounds. With a pastry bag or tube, using the star tip, press rosettes of mayonnaise on the top of the canapés. Freeze on a cooky sheet or whatever fits into your freezer space. When frozen, put the canapés in freezer bags, label, and return to the freezer. *Makes 50 to 60 canapés. Storage time: several months.*

To use: Arrange the frozen canapés on a serving platter and cover with very damp paper towels. Thaw at room temperature for 1½ to 2 hours. Remove towels and serve.

NOTE: These are especially good with Champagne and other wines and with eggnog.

FANCY SEAFOOD RIBBON SANDWICH

1 large round loaf of white bread
6 ounces (180 grams) unsalted butter

FIRST LAYER:

¼ cup (½ deciliter) minced celery
3 ounces (90 grams) red sockeye salmon, canned, or cooked
    fresh salmon
3 ounces (90 grams) unsalted butter
4 stuffed green olives
1 tablespoon mayonnaise
1 teaspoon chopped capers
generous grinding of pepper

Cook celery in a small amount of salted water for 10 minutes.
Drain and cool. Drain the salmon, if canned, and remove the skin
and bones. Mash the salmon and butter in a bowl and add all other
ingredients to it, including the cooled celery. Mix well and set aside.

SECOND LAYER:

3 ounces (90 grams) cream cheese
2 tablespoons (30 milliliters) dairy sour cream
½ teaspoon grated onion
3¾ ounces (106 grams) Danish lumpfish caviar, or real caviar

Mash the cream cheese and add sour cream and grated onion.
When quite soft, gently fold in the caviar. Set aside.

THIRD LAYER:

2¾ ounces (78 grams) slivered blanched almonds
6 large shrimps
2 ounces (60 grams) cream cheese
2 ounces (60 grams) unsalted butter
1 teaspoon anchovy paste

Put the almonds on a cooky sheet and into a 400° F. (205° C.)
oven for 5 to 6 minutes, or until they start to turn golden brown. Do
not let them get too brown or they will taste bitter. Chop them
finely.

Cook the shrimps in boiling salted water for 10 minutes. Drain. Remove the shells and devein the shrimps. Chop them. Mash the cream cheese and add the shrimps, butter, anchovy paste and toasted almonds. Mix well and set aside.

To assemble: Remove all the crust—top, bottom and sides—of the round loaf of bread. Cut the bread horizontally into 4 even slices. Butter the bottom layer. Put the salmon mixture on it and spread it evenly right to the edge. Butter the next bread layer on both sides. Place it on the salmon mixture and see that the edges are lined up. Spread this layer with the caviar mixture. Butter the next bread layer on both sides and place it on the caviar. Put the shrimp mixture on it and spread to the edges. Butter only the bottom of the top layer of bread and place it on the shrimps. Press down firmly to stick all the layers together. Place the ribbon sandwich on a cooky sheet or whatever fits into your freezer space. When frozen, put the ribbon sandwich in a large freezer bag, label, and return to the freezer. *Storage time: 1 to 2 weeks.*

To use: Place the sandwich on a serving platter 24 hours before you need it. Cover with very damp paper towels. Cover towels completely with plastic wrap and put the platter in the refrigerator.

To serve: Sprinkle a few additional chopped, toasted almonds and minced parsley over the top of the sandwich. With a long ser-

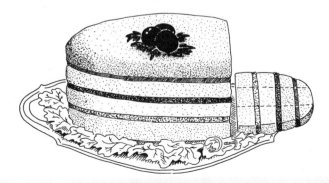

rated knife, cut a ½-inch (1½-centimeter) slice off the side of the sandwich. Cut this slice into 2 or 3 slices, making 2 or 3 servings. Cut another ½-inch (1½-centimeter) slice down through all layers. When this one is cut into slices, it will make 4 or 5 ribbon sandwiches. Continue in this way until everyone is served. *Serves 15 or more people.*

NOTE: If you would like to dress it up a bit more, you could pipe a few rosettes of cream cheese around the edge, with a pastry tube, before freezing or before serving. Also, this ribbon sandwich could be made with a regular loaf of bread, in case you cannot find a round loaf. With a long knife cut off all the crusts from a loaf of unsliced bread. Make 4 even ½-inch (1½-centimeter) slices the long way of the loaf. Layer them just as in the round loaf recipe. The length of bread loaves varies so much that you might need more filling for some loaves. Juniper Hill bread requires almost a double recipe of filling. Assemble it the same way as the round loaf. It may be frosted, top and sides, with a cream-cheese frosting made of 8 ounces (225 grams) cream cheese, softened, 2 tablespoons anchovy paste and enough heavy cream to make it easy to spread. Place on a cooky sheet and freeze as for the round bread sandwich. This makes a very festive presentation.

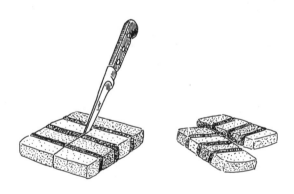

INDEX

Afternoon or Late Night Party
  Menu V, 195
  Menu VI, 195
  Menu VII, 195
Almond(s)
  (and) Blue-Cheese Canapés, 54
  Cheese Almond Crispies, 60
  (and) Cream-Cheese Canapés, 53
  Toasted, 39
Anchovy(ies), 38
  Canapés, Curried, 66
  (and) Caper Canapés, 65
  (and) Caviar Canapés, 74
  in Blue-Cheese Pastry, 64
Artichoke
  Canapés, 144; Variation, 145
  (and) Chicken Canapés, 100
  (and) Cucumber Dip, 145

Bacon Onion Canapés, 136
Balls
  Fish (salt cod), Bite-Size, 66
  Ham Potato, 128
  Ham, Sweet-Sour, 135
Beans in Red Wine, Baked, 185
Beef, Meatballs, Savory, 125

Beef, Roast Beef Slices, 181
Beef, Corned Beef
  Canapés, 127
  Pinwheels, 127
Beef, Dried Beef
  Canapés, 121
  Filling (for Sponge Roll), 124
  Roll, 122, illus 123, 124
Beverages
  Coffee for a Crowd, 200
  Eggnog, 197
  Strawberry Punch, 198
  Tea for a Crowd, 200
Bologna Caviar Canapés, 74
Bread, Juniper Hill, 23

Cake, Pound Cake, Rum and Orange,
  Juniper Hill's, 186
Canapé Bases
  Bread Cases for Cold Hors-
    d'Oeuvre, illus 26, 27
  Bread Rounds and Bases, 24
  Canapé Rounds, 24
  Croustades, Pastry, illus 32, 33
  Croûtes, 28, illus 29
  Melba Toast, Patty's, 30

Canapé Bases (*continued*)
  Toast Cases for Cold Hors-d'Oeuvre, 28
  Toast Cases for Hot Hors-d'Oeuvre, 27, illus 27
  Toast Rounds and Bases, 25
Canapés
  Almond Blue-Cheese, 54
  Almond Cream-Cheese, 53
  Anchovy Caper, 65
  Anchovy, Curried, 66
  Artichoke, 144; Variation, 145
  Bacon Onion, 136
  Blue-Cheese Anchovy, 45
  Blue-Cheese Caviar, 73
  Brie Cheese with Toasted Almonds, 49
  Camembert, Curried, 47
  Caviar, 72
  Caviar Anchovy, 74
  Caviar Bologna, 74
  Cheddar, Hot, 48
  Cheese and Ginger, Hot, 44
  Cheese, Deviled, 56
  Cheese, Juniper Hill's, 52
  Chicken Almond, Cold, 99
  Chicken Almond, Hot, 98
  Chicken Artichoke, 100
  Chicken Chutney, 103
  Chicken, Curried, 102
  Chicken Ham, 104
  Chicken Liver, 107
  Chicken Liver Pâté with Apple, 108
  Chicken Mushroom, 100
  Chicken Mushroom, Cold, 101
  Clam Anchovy, 78
  Clam, Down East, 77
  Corned-Beef, 127
  Crab-Meat, Cold, 85
  Crab-Meat, Hot, 86
  Cucumber Coconut, 203
  Cucumber Mushroom, 146
  Date Orange, 204
  Date Walnut, 205
  Dried-Beef, 121
  Eggplant, 148
  Eggplant Soufflé in Toast Cases, 149
  Eggplant with Pickled Beets, 148

  Green and Red (peppers), 158
  Ham, 134
  Ham, Curried, 132
  Ham-Eggplant, 133
  Ham, with Walnuts, 132
  Herring with Pickled Beets, 68
  Liver (paste), I, 114; II, 115
  Liver Pâté with Almonds, 118
  Liver Pâté with Orange, Hot, 120
  Liver Sausage Spread, 116, illus 116-117
  Liverwurst with Rum-Soaked Raisins, 119
  Lobster Mushroom (cold or hot), 88
  Mushroom Anchovy, 151
  Mustard Sardine, 72
  Onion, Sweet Pickled, Curried, 157
  Oyster, I, 81; II, 82
  Oyster Anchovy, 83
  Oyster Bacon, Hot, 84; Variation, 84
  Oyster-Mushroom, 155
  Pimiento Anchovy, 159
  Pumpernickel Cheese Rounds, 46
  Red Caviar Celery, 75
  Salami, 138
  Salami with Orange Butter, 137
  Sardine, Hot, 70
  Sardine, Souffléed, 71
  Sausage and Green-Pepper, 139
  Shrimp, 89
  Shrimp Mushroom, 90
  Shrimp Pâté II, 93
  Smoked Baby Clam, Hot, 78
  Smoked Mussels with Cream Cheese, 79
  Smoked Salmon, 69
  Tongue, 134
Caviar
  (and) Anchovy Canapés, 74
  (and) Blue-Cheese Canapés, 73
  (and) Bologna Canapés, 74
  Canapés, 72
  Red Caviar Celery Canapés, 75
Champagne Party, 194
Cheese
  Ball, Juniper Hill, 55
  (and) Black-Olive Roll, 57

Puffs with Blue-Cheese Cream, 58
Pumpernickel Cheese Rounds, 46
Wafers, 58
Cheese, Blue Cheese
(and) Almond Canapés, 54
and Anchovy Canapés, 45
(and) Caviar Canapés, 73
Cream, 58
Pastry I and II, 36
Cheese, Brie Cheese
with Toasted Almonds (canapés),
49
Cheese, Camembert
Canapés, Curried, 47
Cheese, Cheddar
(and) Almond Crispies, 60
Canapés, Hot, 48
and Ginger Canapés, Hot, 44
Twists, 59, illus 59
Cheese, Cream Cheese, 38
(and) Almond Canapés, 53
Canapés, Deviled, 56
(and) Chutney Ribbon Sandwiches,
201, illus 202
Curried Anchovy Canapés, 66
Cheese, Edam or Gouda
Stuffed, 50, illus 51
Stuffed, with Pickled Onions, 51
Chicken
(and) Almond Canapés, Cold, 99
(and) Almond Canapés, Hot, 98
(and) Artichoke Canapés, 100
Canapés, Curried, 102
(and) Chutney Canapés, 103
Filling (for Sponge Roll), 124
(and) Ham Canapés, 104
and Ham Rolls, 135
(and) Ham Turnovers, 105
(and) Mushroom Canapés, 100
(and) Mushroom Canapés, Cold,
101
Pinwheels, 106, illus 106
Chicken Liver
Canapés, 107
Pâté with Apple, 108
Pâté with Brandied Raisins, 109
Clam(s)
(and) Anchovy Canapés, 78
in Patty Shells, 76

Smoked Baby Clam Canapés, Hot,
78
Spread and Canapés, Down East,
77
Cocktail-Buffet
Menu I, 176
Menu II, 176
Menu III, 177
Menu IV, 177
table setting, illus 170-171
Cocktail Sauce, 165
Coconut Cucumber Canapés or
Sandwiches, 203
Coconut, Toasted, 39
Cod, Salt, Fish Balls, Bite-Size, 66
Coffee for a Crowd, 200
Coleslaw, Down East, 178
Crab Meat
Canapés, Cold, 85
Canapés, Hot, 86
Patties, Spicy, 86
Turnovers, Hot, 87
Cranberry Orange Relish, 182
Cream Sauce, 154, 179
Croustades, Pastry, illus 32, 33
Croûtes, 28, illus 29
Cucumber Coconut Canapés or
Sandwiches, 203
Cucumber Mushroom Canapés, 146
Curried
Anchovy Canapés, 66
Camembert Canapés, 47
Chicken Canapés, 102
Ham and Egg Spread, 130
Ham Canapés, 132
Sweet Pickled Onion Canapés, 157

Date Orange Canapés, 204
Date Walnut Canapés, 205
Deviled Cheese Canapés, 56
Dips, 38
Artichoke Cucumber, 145
Liver Sausage, 116
Oyster, 80
Smoked Mussels with Cream
Cheese, 79
Down East Clam Spread and Canapés, 77
Down East Coleslaw, 178

Egg and Ham Spread, Curried, 130
Eggnog, 197
Eggnog Party, 196
  Menu VIII, 197
Eggplant
  Canapés, 148
  Caviar, 147
  Soufflé in Toast Cases, 149
  with Pickled Beets, 148
Egg yolks for garnish, 39
Equipment, 10

Filling
  Chicken (for Sponge Roll), 124
  Dried-Beef (for Sponge Roll), 124
  Lemon (for Pie), 187
  Shrimp (for Sponge Roll), 124
Fish Balls, Bite-Size (salt cod), 66
Fish, *see also names of fish*
Freezing hors-d'oeuvre, 21

Garnishes, 38
Green and Red Canapés, 158

Ham
  Balls, Sweet-Sour, 135
  Canapés, 134
  Canapés, Curried, 132
  Canapés with Walnuts, 132
  (and) Chicken Canapés, 104
  and Chicken Rolls, 135
  (and) Chicken Turnovers, 105
  (and) Chutney Rolls, 129
  -Eggplant Canapés, 133
  and Egg Spread, Curried, 130
  Pinwheels, 131
  (and) Potato Balls, 128
  Slices, Baked, 183
Herring with Pickled Beets, 68
Horseradish Cream, 168

Jane's Party Pâté, 120
Juniper Hill Bread, 23
Juniper Hill Cheese Ball, 55
Juniper Hill Meat Puffs and Pin-
  wheels, 126
Juniper Hill's Cheese Spread and
  Canapés, 52

Juniper Hill's Rum and Orange
  Pound Cake, 186

Lemon Meringue Pie, 186
Liver, Chicken
  Canapés, 107
  Pâté with Apple, 108
  Pâté with Brandied Raisins, 109
Liver Paste
  Canapés I, 114; II, 115
  Jane's Party Pâté, 120
  Pâté Canapés with Almonds, 118
  Pâté Canapés with Orange, Hot,
  120
Liver Sausage
  Spread or Dip, 116, illus 116-117
Liverwurst
  with Rum-Soaked Raisins, 119
Lobster Mushroom Canapés (cold or
  hot), 88
Lobster-Stuffed Mushrooms, 154

Meat
  Pinwheels, Juniper Hill, 126
  Puffs, Juniper Hill, 126
  see also Beef; Ham; Liver; Bacon;
  Salami; Sausage
Meatballs, Savory, 125
Menus
  Afternoon or Late Night Party, V,
  195; VI, 195; VII, 195
  Cocktail-Buffet, I, 176; II, 176; III,
  177; IV, 177
  Eggnog Party, VIII, 197
  Punch Party, IX, 199; X, 199
  Tea or Coffee Party, XI, 201; XII,
  201
Meringue, 188
Metrics, 17
  Conversion Table, 18
Mushroom(s)
  (and) Anchovy Canapés, 151
  Cucumber Mushroom Canapés,
  146
  Lobster-Stuffed, 154
  Oyster-Stuffed, 155
  Sausage-Stuffed, 156
  (and) Shrimp Canapés, 90
  Stuffed with Celery, 153

Stuffed with Chicken Livers, 152
Stuffed with Ham, 153
Turnovers, 150, illus 151
Mussels, Smoked, with Cream Cheese, Spread or Dip, 79
Mustard
  -Caper Sauce, 167
  (and) Sardine Canapés, 72
  Sauce, 166

Noodle Onion Sour-Cream Casserole, 183

Olive, Black-Olive Cheese Roll, 57
Onion
  Bacon Onion Canapés, 136
  Rings, Batter-Fried, 184
  (and) Sour-Cream Noodle Casserole, 183
  Sweet Pickled, Curried, Canapés, 157
Orange Cranberry Relish, 182
Orange and Rum Pound Cake, Juniper Hill's, 186
Oyster
  (and) Anchovy Canapés, 83
  (and) Bacon Canapés, Hot, 84; Variation, 84
  Canapés I, 81; II, 82
  Dip, 80
  -Stuffed Mushrooms, 155

Parsley, 38
Party Pizza, 160, illus 161
Pastry, Basic
  Blue-Cheese Pastry I and II, 36
  Flaky Pastry, 30, illus 31
  Pastry Croustades, illus 32, 33
  Pastry for Lemon Meringue Pie, 187
  Pastry Puffs (Petits Choux), 34
  Patty Shells, 37
  Tartlet Shells for Hot and Cold Hors-d'Oeuvre, 33
Pastry Hors-d'Oeuvre
  Anchovies in Blue-Cheese Pastry, 64
  Cheddar Twists, 59, illus 59
  Cheese Almond Crispies, 60

Cheese Puffs with Blue-Cheese Cream, 58
Cheese Wafers, 58
Clams in Patty Shells, 76
Crab-Meat Patties, Spicy, 86
Meat Puffs, Juniper Hill, 126
Salmon in Pastry, 178, illus 179-181
Salmon Pinwheels, 69
Sausage and Green-Pepper Patties, 139
Shrimp Mushroom Canapés, 90
Pâté
  Chicken Liver, with Apple, 108
  Chicken Liver, with Brandied Raisins, 109
  Jane's Party Pâté, 120
  Liver (paste), Canapés with Almonds, 118
  Liver (paste), Canapés with Orange, Hot, 120
  Shrimp, I, 92; II, 93
Patty's Melba Toast, 30
Peppers, Green and Red Canapés, 158
Petits Choux (Pastry Puffs), 34
Pie, Lemon Meringue, 186
Pimiento Anchovy Canapés, 159
Pinwheels, illus 106
  Chicken, 106
  Ham, 131
  Meat, Juniper Hill, 126
  Salmon, 69
Pizza, Party, 160, illus 161
Punch Party, 198
  Menu IX, 199
  Menu X, 199

Raisin Sauce, 167
Raisins, Brandied, 40
Relish, Orange Cranberry, 182
Rémoulade Sauce, 169
Rolls or Pinwheels without pastry
  Corned-Beef, 127
  Ham and Chicken, 135
  Ham Chutney, 129

Salami Canapés, 138
Salami with Orange Butter, 137

Salmon
 in Pastry, 178, illus 179-181
 Pinwheels, 69
 Smoked, Canapés, 69
Sandwiches
 Cheese Chutney Ribbon, 201, illus
  202
 Cucumber Coconut, 203
 Seafood Ribbon, Fancy, 206, illus
  207, 208
Sardine
 Canapés, Hot, 70
 Canapés, Souffléed, 71
 (and) Mustard Canapés, 72
Sauce
 Cocktail, 165
 Cream, 154, 179
 Horseradish Cream, 168
 Mustard, 166
 Mustard-Caper, 167
 Raisin, 167
 Rémoulade, 169
 Savory, 166
 Shrimp Butter, 91
 Sweet-Sour, 168
Sausage and Green-Pepper Patties,
 139
Sausage-Stuffed Mushrooms, 156
Savory Meatballs, 125
Savory Sauce, 166
Seafood Ribbon Sandwich, Fancy,
 206, illus 207, 208
Shrimp
 Butter, 91
 Canapés, 89
 Filling (for Sponge Roll), 124
 (and) Mushroom Canapé, 90
 Pâté I, 92; II, 93
Soufflé, Eggplant, in Toast Cases, 149

Spinach-Filled Toast Cases, 162
Sponge Roll, 122, illus 123
Spreads, 38
 Cheese, Deviled, 56
 Cheese, Juniper Hill's, 52
 Clam, Down East, 77
 Crab-Meat, Cold, 85
 Cucumber Mushroom, 146
 Curried Camembert, 47
 Eggplant Caviar, 147
 Ham and Egg, Curried, 130
 Ham-Eggplant, 133
 Liver Pâté, with Almonds, 118
 Liverwurst with Rum-Soaked
  Raisins, 119
 Oyster Anchovy, 83
 Oyster Canapés I, 81; II, 82
 Pimiento Anchovy, 159
 Smoked Mussels with Cream
  Cheese, 79
Strawberry Punch, 198
Sweet-Sour Ham Balls, 135
Sweet-Sour Sauce, 168

Tea for a Crowd, 200
Tea or Coffee Party, 200
 Menu XI, 201
 Menu XII, 201
Thawing bread canapés, 21
Thawing toast canapés or turnovers,
 22
Toast Cases, Spinach-Filled, 162
Toast, Melba, Patty's, 30
Tongue Canapés, 134
Turkey Slices, 182
Turnovers, illus 151
 Chicken Ham, 105
 Crab-Meat, Hot, 87
 Mushroom, 150